THE BEST OF TIMES, THE WORST OF TIMES
The Paradox of Today
AN EXPLANATION

JOHN REED

UMBRIA PRESS

Copyright © John Reed 2023

John Reed has asserted his right under
the Copyright, Design and Patents Act
to be identified as the author of this work.

Umbria Press
London SW15 5DP
www.umbriapress.co.uk

Printed by Ashford Colour Press Ltd
Gosport PO13 0FW
www.ashfordps.co.uk

ISBN 978 1 910074 46 6

*To Roberto & Vikki
with much love,
John*

THE BEST OF TIMES, THE WORST OF TIMES

– (Dominique's artwork on cover)

To
Liam Kai Reed

"Periodically in Western history twilight ages make their appearance. Processes of decline and erosion of institutions are more evident than those of genesis and development. Something like a vacuum obtains in the moral order for large numbers of people. Human loyalties uprooted from accustomed soil can be seen tumbling across the landscape with no scheme or larger purpose to fix them. Individualism reveals itself less as achievement and enterprise than as egoism and mere performance. Retreat from major to minor, from the noble to the trivial, the communal to the personal and from the objective to the subjective. There is a widely expressed sense of degradation of values and corruption of culture. The sense of estrangement from community is strong."

Robert Nisbet (1913-1996)

"The human is a knot of contradictions and opposing drives: faithlessness and mysticism; logic and imagination. We feed on exact science as much as we do on myths, on fictions and fabulations. We can die for others or let them perish in the cold; we can create extraordinary things only to enjoy their utter destruction; human society can be paradise and hell at one and the same time."

Costica Bradatan

"The so-called death of God, after which everything is supposedly permitted, has not worked out so well for human society. Without a relation to the infinite, human beings will tend to lose their bearings. The vast majority, cast adrift in a universe without intrinsic meaning, will experience a spiritual vertigo that is the source of countless social ills. If we desire genuine well-being, both individual and social, we must find some way to renew our connection with the infinite. To put it another way, we need to recover our souls."

William Ophuls

Contents

	Introduction	11
1	Social Media. A Poisoned Chalice	27
2	Capitalism. Friend or Foe?	40
3	Civilization in Jeopardy	62
4	Finance. The Day of Reckoning Approaches	81
5	Spirituality. An Uneven Trajectory	94
6	Hope	111
	Epilogue	142
	Acknowledgements	149

Introduction

The purpose of this book is to enquire into the puzzling disconnection between all the 'wonders' that modernity has bestowed on the world (but more particularly on advanced industrial societies) raising living standards to unimaginable levels compared with anytime in the past, and the climate of disenchantment that has also set in, fostering widespread discouragement and a pandemic of depression and mental illness. What can explain the striking contradiction between what we have been conditioned to expect from the spectacular progress of the last seventy years and the climate of negativity that co-exists with that euphoria? Is it just a question of haves and have nots? Not entirely.

It is a foundational belief in the West that economic growth is the driver of 'progress'. Hand in hand with this credo comes a largely unquestioned faith that personal fulfillment and collective well-being is the reward for ever higher standards of living and to a large extent that has been the case until recent times. In 1980 over forty per cent of humanity lived at subsistence levels of poverty. Today it is less than ten per cent. In the same time-period, life expectancy has made a huge leap while illiteracy has halved. The world generates as much economic output in a month today as it did in an entire year in 1950. All these positive developments belong on the credit side of the ledger. On the debit side, we find growing social and political instability, unprecedented levels of inequality, a growing problem of depression and mental illness, the alarming rise of far-right and authoritarian political parties , the weakening of democracy and now, the most destructive war in Europe since World War Two – making people question the benefit of economic improvement alone.

What went wrong?

Many will tell you that nothing went wrong; we are far better off today than at any time in the past by any metric you care to choose and that this is just a temporary setback soon to be remedied by some needed adjustments and, of course, further inputs of economic growth. Taking the longer view, a smaller group of resolute optimists place all their faith on technological innovation. Those are the people who subscribe to extravagant fantasies such as the prospect of a bio-engineered, trans-human world of AI (known as the 'Singularity') – an indication, in my view, of how the physical has dangerously surpassed the metaphysical in human life and how little consideration is given to the soul. By aiming to recreate the human by non-human means, the Singularity represents the technological dehumanization of life in its purist form.

There is an ominous tendency in this kind of thinking to believe that the fate of humanity should be in the hands of a capable few who would use AI in the best interest of the human race. Klaus Schwab, the leader of The Word Economic Forum (WEF) promises a 'Great Reset' achieved through technological precision, bio-engineering, centralized management of the worlds resources, the merger of human and artificial intelligence and the monopolization of government power by a small professional class with the required expertise.

They draw inspiration for the model of the future from the Platonic ideal of the city-state ruled by a 'philosopher king' with no attempt to determine whether such 'philosopher kings' actually exist and if they do, how can they be identified and designated. The obvious flaw in this theory as applied to modern times is that, although aspiring 'kings' are many, 'philosopher kings' – meaning wise and enlightened servants of the people, are nowhere to be found - not now or at any time in the past. And yet, one without the other is just a prescription for the form of tyranny we are well acquainted with and that the world has suffered from since its beginnings.

It is worth noting that by doubling down on economic growth and technology, Einstein's famous definition of insanity (repeating the same mistakes but expecting different results) is being demonstrated as never before. Why? Because the cause of a problem (unbridled growth) cannot simultaneously be its solution. As author and social critic, Charles Hugh-Smith stated: "The unencumbered realist concludes that there are no solutions with a status quo structure that is itself the problem." Is this an admission that we don't have the answers? I believe so. Not only do we not have the answers, but we don't seem able to envisage any options either. The modern world has become a one-dimensional, one-directional force of economic and technological growth. However, there is a fundamental difference this time. That particular social and economic dynamic is coming at the cost of a marked deterioration of the human psyche. This calls for an entirely new conceptual approach to the problem. It's no coincidence, perhaps, that this development highlights another of Einstein's notable insights, namely that: "A problem cannot be resolved at the level of thinking that created it".

At present, the only 'level of thinking' we are capable of – instrumental reason, linear thinking and pragmatism – is clearly not up to the task. Unsurprisingly, these well-worn methods continue to meet with mixed results; we win one battle only to lose another and can never seem to break out of the familiar patterns from the past. Again, the malaise of the spirit we see today cannot respond well to these methods because it is a direct consequence of them. As a result, a sense of socio-political bankruptcy hovers over society. Bereft of inspiration, political parties of the left, right or centre succeed each other with great regularity, proposing policies that become progressively more extreme in their search for answers. When, in their turn, these policies also fail, democracy comes under fire as people grasp at desperate and often violent means to correct the situation. Instability then becomes endemic.

For example, the newly elected prime minister of Great Britain, Liz Truss, has just resigned after forty-five days in office (and a stunning reversal of policy) with the new PM to be the fifth since 2015 (unprecedented in Tory history). Italy has just elected its seventy-third government since the war. Israel has had five elections in four years. Netanyahu has been in and out of office no less than three times of late and has been prime minister a total of six times. With the recent alliance with the far-right, the threat to Israeli democracy has become very real. The Iranian people who welcomed the mullahs forty-five years ago now want to expel them. Xi Jinping has reverted to Mao-like control of China while Vladimir Putin, is waging a devastating but old-fashioned war of territorial aggrandizement the like of which we haven't seen since the Second World War. Brazil is in the midst of a hotly contested election where a former (discredited) leftist president is trying to oust a rightest president with authoritarian leanings.

Politics in the US has turned into a civil war between two hostile and intransigent political parties, one of whom is sure to contest the results of the next general election. With a growing number of countries subject to authoritarian or semi-authoritarian rule, the limits of liberal democracy are being tested. Authoritarian regimes are waiting to see what transpires in Ukraine. If Putin's war is successful, some will be emboldened to follow his example.

For this reason, the need for the more evolved level of thinking that Einstein was referring to, has never seemed more urgent than today.

But how to do this? What kind of resources do we possess that can bring this about?

In an attempt to measure the full extent of mankind's potential, the scientific community has conducted exhaustive studies of the mind. The human brain has been dissected and investigated from every angle while the question 'what is consciousness?' has been endlessly debated by psychologists. In spite of these endeavours, human consciousness remains largely 'terra incognita'. "The greatest mystery in the world is consciousness", Eckhart Tolle tells us. The reason is simple. Science has no portal into the psycho/spiritual dimension of our beings which is the essential domain of consciousness. Science does not (by definition) recognize spirituality because its existence cannot be proved. It was outlawed from serious intellectual inquiry by Descartes, Darwin and the Rationalists a long time ago for the reasons that make science what it is.

As a result, spirituality, wrongly associated with conventional 'religion', has been relegated to the margins of what is deemed real and practicable in a modern technological world. Its more visible practitioners (the 'New Age' community) have done little to change that view. There is, however, substantial evidence to support the existence of a spiritual reality. One irrefutable fact that the scientific community, atheists and non-believers in general have never been able to reconcile is that a long-standing and distinguished lineage of some of the greatest thinkers that have ever lived had one thing in common; they all believed in a spiritual reality. Despite this, the needle hardly moves. Science and technology with its sheer physicality, rationality and practicality has become the religion of our time. Like the once-held belief that the earth was flat, with the exception of a convinced minority (to which I belong), spiritual beliefs are considered outdated and irrelevant by the vast majority of mankind.

However, science can also be accused of hubris because the mantle of infallibility that it attributes to itself is not entirely justified. *The Science Delusion* by Cambridge biochemist Rupert Sheldrake, a timely treatise on fallible human hubris exposes the truth that, no matter how facts-based and empirical science is in its methodology, scientific knowledge remains provisional. The recent 'double-slit' experiment of quantum mechanics (of which I understand nothing) apparently contradicts the laws of physics considered absolute fact for hundreds of years. Among multiple other illustrations of the limits of human knowledge, Sheldrake also points out that ninety-five per cent of the world remains 'dark matter', unexplained by the human mind. Under the circumstances, it would be reasonable to expect some humility from the scientific community or, at the very least, a greater openness to the question of spirituality.

In return, readers must wonder if the premises of science have proved to be shaky, what permanence or solidity can be attributed to spiritual principles? How do they stand up to the test of time? I can only answer that by saying that there is a fundamental difference between the two. Spirituality is first and foremost experiential not interpretative. It does not attempt to explain the existence of 'God', grace, faith or enlightenment. Why? Because there is need to understand the mechanics of higher consciousness when its validity is to be found in the EXPERIENCE itself. The basic premise of spirituality is that the workings of the human spirit are beyond the comprehension of the human mind. Any attempt to analyze it scientifically is futile. Another important consideration is that, while the brain and the capacity of the human mind has evolved massively over time, testimonies of spiritual experience going back thousands of years suggests that the psycho/spiritual condition of humanity has remained remarkably stable over the same period.

As social scientist Jonah Goldberg puts it: "For all intents and purposes, human nature holds constant as the world changes around us. This is a truth better comprehended through literature than from science."

Referring back to the message of the Buddha (600BC), Taoist writings of Lao Tzu (500BC) or Chuang Tzu (350 BC) we see that core aspects of human nature – greed, pride, ambition etc. – manifested themselves in a very similar manner in ancient times as it does today. Widely disparate spiritual traditions were grouped together and labeled *The Perennial Philosophy* by Aldous Huxley because he recognized an underlying similarity between them with regards to how they perceived and addressed human nature. Those aspects of human behaviour have remained largely constant. In more recent times, there is no better testament of how little human nature changes, than the plays of Shakespeare. The fact that we can so easily identify with the qualities and failings of his characters, as well as the moral climate of the time, is what makes Shakespeare an unparalleled chronicler of the human condition. The great novelists of the eighteen and nineteenth centuries did much the same. This would suggest that while the 'outer', physical aspects of human existence have progressed significantly - who wears armour, travels on horseback or lives in unheated castles today? - the 'inner', psycho/spiritual condition of mankind has barely budged. This imbalance, I would suggest, is at the heart of many of the problems we face today.

By means of experiments such as the monitoring of brain waves during meditation, science has gamely tried to investigate matters pertaining to the human spirit though nothing conclusive has been achieved or ever can be achieved. All attempts to bring spirituality into the mainstream of human thought will be futile until we are able to CONCEPTUALIZE beyond the limitations and straitjacket of empiricism and reason - which, if it were to happen, would itself be a spiritual endeavour. In the words of William Ophuls: "The problems created by instrumental rationality will not be solved by it, but rather a vision of a nobler future that appeals to Pascal's 'reason of the heart'."

In the meantime, the all-important question of human 'consciousness' is worth closer examination.

Simplifying greatly, I shall advance the view (heresy to most people) that our moral and psychological condition depends on the quality of our consciousness – there being not one but multiple layers of consciousness. These layers can be broken down into several categories. The lower states of consciousness (our 'normal' condition, say) operate at a practical and rational level. It's what science identifies as 'waking consciousness' (as opposed to being asleep) and the only form of consciousness it recognizes. It is also in this state that most of us interact with the world. A range, however, exists within that category. At the very lowest levels of consciousness, you will find people who are primal in their conduct and instincts. Morality, in the traditional sense of the word, is absent. This is the realm of criminals and psychopaths that can range from rapacious businessmen to men like Vladimir Putin. At the upper level of the same (lower consciousness) range you get very exceptional individuals like Mandela, Schweitzer or Gorbachev. Decent and well-meaning people, the vast majority of mankind, are somewhere in between.

Higher states of consciousness, on the other hand, are something quite distinct. They work on a much finer energetic frequency that affords deeper insights into the psycho/spiritual reality of life and are very rare. Again, these perceptions can vary in depth and intensity and encompass a narrower range of people than is the case with lower states of consciousness. The higher end of this range would include individuals of an exceptionally rare spiritual stature like Plato, Lao Tzu and Siddhartha Gautama (the Buddha) as well as St Francis or mystics such a Meister Eckhart (Jesus Christ belongs in a supra-human category that I would not be capable of defining). At the lower end of this range, you would find spiritually oriented thinkers, writers and teachers such as Jung, Tolstoy, Gandhi and the Dalai Lama or even mystical poets such as Wordsworth or Blake. Very few people we would consider 'normal', even those with spiritual leanings, would belong in the higher consciousness category at any level.

A higher or lower level of consciousness is not, I hasten to add, a question of greater or lesser degrees of 'intelligence' as we know it - a person can split the atom, invent the internet and transplant hearts in a lower state of consciousness. In fact, most 'brilliant' people (in the normally accepted meaning of the word) are in the lower consciousness category. The two levels of consciousness do not operate on the same continuum. Higher consciousness demonstrates an altogether different TYPE of intelligence that combines more evolved forms of intuition, instinct and revelation. In a purely clinical sense, psychologists have long acknowledged that different states of consciousness exist but have no means of understanding what a higher state of consciousness consists of or how to access it. This is and has always been the domain of spirituality.

So what relevance does all this have to the state of the world today?

A great deal, as it happens. Between what science can recognize and what it can't, a gaping void exists in our understanding of what the full potential of a human being can be. It is important to recognize that much that is happening in the world today results from the fact that our civilization was largely constructed WITHOUT this understanding, that is, in lower states of consciousness with a minimal influence from higher states. This imperatively must change as we go forward. Building the modern world while lacking some of the higher faculties a human being can possess goes a long way to explaining the profound and endemic anomalies that have weighed on conditions of life on the planet until now.

But for some historical context, we must go back some 400 years.

The man mostly responsible for the direction the world has taken in its evolution towards modernity was French philosopher René Descartes, whose legacy to Western civilization is based on a colossal error. His famed proclamation, 'I think therefore I am', by opening the floodgates of a purely rational and empirical interpretation of reality, prevented the transcendent dimension of humanity from taking root (or even be understood), replacing it with a secular and mechanistic vision of life that was entirely lopsided. Descartes's error, alas, was never corrected and has held sway ever since. As a result, reason and self-interest have shaped the world we live in exclusively. What we are seeing is the inexorable and LOGICAL outcome of Descartes's misguided views re-enforced at every turn by the powerful dynamic of human self-interest (egoism).

So, yes, from the cornucopia of material progress at our disposal, modernity has given us (some of us, that is) the internet, gadget-laden homes, electric cars, space travel, ever-smarter smartphones and so on. But it has also given us a dysfunctional capitalist system, an unacceptable divide between the have and the have nots, a mental health pandemic, worldwide political instability, galloping inflation, the ravages of climate change and a cruel and destructive war in Europe – hardly the outcome we might have expected from so much 'progress'.

One further consideration. Even in the darkest moments of history the world remained buoyed up by hope and the expectation that if we could turn the corner on the major event of the time, be it the World Wars or Soviet Communism, we could go on to build a freer, more just, peaceful and prosperous world. As an expression of this belief in the future we created institutions such as the UN, the IMF and The World Bank and so on. For many people such expectations are now gone and it's not just climate change that is responsible for that shift. There is the feeling that we have come to 'the end of history', not the utopia of liberal democracy that Francis Fukuyama once famously proclaimed – but the exhaustion of hope itself.

What then can be done?

Again, I can only repeat what I have already said. The major obstacle to change is the blind spot in our understanding of the human potential locked up in the spiritual core of each one of us. It is our spiritual nature that determines who we are, not our intelligence, talents, social standing or physical attributes. Without self-awareness, we are empty shells no matter how generously nature has endowed us with such qualities. The underlying insecurity that can linger in the shadows of some people's lives, even those who have been given the most, only serves to confirm this. The fact is a pauper is a king when he is spiritually whole in the same way that a king is a pauper when he isn't. And we live in an increasingly pauperized world. Qualities vital to the survival of our civilization such as empathy, humility, forbearance, tolerance, care and compassion – largely absent from our lives today – come from that same unique source. Martin Luther King's most famous speech began with the words: 'I have a dream'. Is it conceivable that, as individuals, we too can 'have a dream' and acquire a spiritual vision of what life can be beyond the moral void we have created for ourselves?

If this were so, every aspect of life would change. The structures, organization and the entire trajectory of the modern world would alter. No amount of political will, force or legislation can achieve this. We have tried them all. Today, we are at a critical inflection point. The spectacular gains that modernity has bestowed on us, for lack of a moderating force that only wisdom can provide, fester and are infecting our civilization like a deadly virus. Our moral immune system is collapsing, and we have become uniquely vulnerable. Everywhere you look entropic forces are at work, not only socially, economically and politically but, most importantly, in the diminishment of our souls. We are disintegrating from within and only a tiny minority of us are sounding the alarm. The rest go about their lives as though this party will never end.

At this late hour, is it possible to reverse the situation and bring about a psycho/spiritual rebirth on the scale and magnitude that is needed?

The purpose of this book is to examine that question.

I
SOCIAL MEDIA, A POISONED CHALICE

It is not sufficiently acknowledged nowadays that social media is an unparalleled plague that has crept up on us surreptitiously, but now has a tight grip on the minds and spirit of billions of people throughout the world. Not only has the use of social media withered our attention span in a bewilderingly short space of time but it has managed to alter the entire nature of communication between people. Whereas in the past, we communicated using our minds, senses and emotions, the intercession of technology has changed all that. We now relate to each other through a technological prism that has filtered out the direct quality of the former experience and introduced a mechanical intermediary (the mobile phone/computer) that renders the experience impersonal and distant without people being fully aware that this has happened.

How has the combination of distance and technology been able to alter the very nature of human contact? The written (texted) word has bypassed the expression of emotion that only physical proximity confers. Some view this as a form of freedom. It demands less of them, permitting a reduced engagement of real feelings, a barrier behind which some people feel safe. Unfortunately, this new freedom is no freedom at all since the vacuum arising from the lack of genuine engagement is filled with facile, less meaningful, less authentic and more trivial forms of interaction that create an addiction where none existed before.

According to Scott Galloway, who assembled a treasure trove of information in his data-filled book *Adrift*, a 2020 study to investigate the extent of the addiction found that 96% of Gen Z Americans unlock their phones no less than EIGHTY times a day and won't go to the bathroom without them! There also seems to be no easy way for a young person to simply opt out of the use of social media either. Studies reveal that a young person who isn't on social media is belittled and ostracized by his peers as though there was something wrong with him or her (causing serious psychological repercussions if they try).

The young, however, are not alone in their vulnerability to the corrosive effects of social media. Daily phone use by all Americans has increased at the astonishing rate of 25% a year since 2010. Today, an average American spends 4 hours and 23 minutes a day on his or her mobile device. So indispensable, pressing and all-important has the use of social media become in the lives of these people (or so it is perceived) that phones have now become an extension of their identities, Scott Galloway informs us, another way of saying that their genuine identities have all but disappeared. This is eerily reminiscent of the lobotomized denizens of Aldous Huxley's *Brave New World* who ingest a soporific drug distributed by the authorities that makes them compliant and contented at the price of ceasing to exist as individuals. Mind you, if this hadn't already been the case to some degree, social media could not have had the effect it has had in so short a time.

Facebook and Instagram, however, by becoming the largely contrived and showcased substitute for what people would like their lives to be, take these susceptibilities to a whole different level. Where a shaky identity might have existed beforehand, the tidal wave of 'other directedness' unleashed by these platforms would undermine all but those with the strongest psyche. Social media feeds on insecurity. It is both the reason people tend to use these platforms as well as the consequence of doing so. Again, the fact that personal insecurity existed on a significant scale beforehand greatly facilitated its rapid development.

Twitter, as the childish sound of the word indicates, offers up the seemingly harmless image of the little yellow bird in the Warner Bros cartoons tweeting away sweetly. Alas, nothing could be further from the truth. Twitter is another toxic platform used by Uber drivers to presidents to communicate with the world. Here again, the tendency is to make short, superficial, often imprecise but sometimes pseudo-weighty statements as a substitute for serious forms of communication. This was Donald Trump's favoured form of communication, and he used it ceaselessly and with great effect until, far too late in the game, he was banned from it. Under the control of Elon Musk, this is no longer the case, it seems.

Now, some might wish to argue that shallow behaviour was not born with the internet and the iPhone and that social media has only given it greater expression and could be considered relatively harmless. Again, that's not the case. First of all, it's no coincidence that the timing of the mental health crisis in America correlates almost perfectly with the smartphone's use as a substitute for in-person socialization. It is quite possible that Mark Zuckerberg, Jack Dorsey and the others had no idea what monsters they had created (at first) or could have envisaged the ensuing ramifications. Nonetheless, it would not be an exaggeration to say that the (unwitting) emergence of social media is one of the most unanticipated but momentous developments in modern times that took everyone by surprise. It is the socio-cultural equivalent of the invention of the atom bomb with the difference that the bomb, mercifully, has only been used once while the fallout from social media is having its deleterious effect on billions of people every moment of every day everywhere. It doesn't destroy us physically, but it eats away at our moral and spiritual individuality until there's little left of us – and that's precisely what we see today.

It also gives people the false sense of belonging to a community (a vital need that has all but disappeared in modern societies) but does so in an illusory manner. *The New York Times* editorialist Ross Douthat observed: "It's a place where people form communities and alliances, nurture friendships and sexual relationships, yell and flirt, cheer and pray – a place they don't just visit but inhabit." This is understandable. Community serves an important purpose provided it is authentic. Social media offers only an illusory variant of it. The thirst for a meaningful connection to others is not assuaged. The persistence of those unmet needs has had a significant effect on mental health.

Let me briefly outline some of the most negative consequences.

The first and most significant victim of social media is TRUTH, our umbilical connection to reality and the mother's milk of human interaction. How did this come about? As Scott Galloway informs us, the first victim of the emergence of Facebook and Google was traditional journalism. In 2008, U.S newspapers generated $38 billion in advertising revenue. By 2020 it had shrunk to $9 billion, a record low. With dwindling revenues there were fewer journalists. The number of employees from newspapers to television fell from 114,000 in 2008 to 85,000 in 2020. "If the number of American journalists served as a proxy measurement for our nation's collective truth, the truth was in sharp decline," stated Galloway. As Twitter and other platforms became a source of 'news' for millions (7 in 10 American Twitter users say they get the news on the site) veracity of information could no longer be relied on.

As other social media platforms like Instagram came to the party, attention spans shrunk even further. By 2014, 55% of website visits lasted less than 15 seconds, according to Scott Galloway. This had distinctly harmful consequences on news outlets. To maintain advertising revenues, they were obliged to seize on to and hold our attention by concentrating on sensational news stories and, more particularly, headlines. As Galloway reports: "In the previous era of news, the only trackable performance metric was print sales, but the internet allows journalistic institutions to measure what drives readership down to the individual headline. It soon became clear that virality was directly correlated with emotion: the most popular headlines are ones that disturb, shock and enrage us." Wharton Business School researchers confirm this by discovering that the three principal characteristics ensuring maximum virality were anxiety (up by 21%), awe (up by 30%) with anger leading the pack with an increase of a whopping 43%.

These developments saw the emergence of a whole new form of news, one determined entirely by what panders to the basest forms of human emotion and not traditional newsworthiness or the maintenance of editorial standards, as in the past. Between 2010 and 2015, Twitter's monthly user base grew from 10 to 300 million. While journalists were being forced to dramatize the news, "For Twitter users it meant making it up. An MIT study examined a data set of 126,000 tweets. The time taken for falsehood to reach 1,500 people, they found, was SIX times shorter than it was for the truth to do the same. Meanwhile, 7 in 10 US adult Twitter users say they get news on the site" according to Galloway. This is an absolutely seismic shift in the way news is gathered, interpreted and distributed but it perfectly illustrates the kind of divergence that is at the origin of the great 'contradiction' we are living through today. On the one hand we have greater access to news and information than at any time in the past, on the other, never has that news and information been less reliable or true!

Truth, in the meantime, is not a luxury. It is the essential underpinning of TRUST. Lose one and you will lose the other. Trust is painstakingly hard to build but can be lost very swiftly. No social or political system can operate effectively without it. Democracy is founded on trust. Law and Order, too. In a personal relationship, the breakdown of trust is invariably irretrievable. According to Derek Thompson writing for *The Atlantic*, in 2022, the medical journal *The Lancet* published an analysis of which variables best predicted the rates of Covid infection across 177 countries. Apart from wealth, one of the most powerful variables was TRUST in government among the public. "Trust is a shared resource that enables networks of people to do collectively what individual actors cannot," the authors of *The Lancet* paper wrote. By sacrificing truth, we destroy trust. The immediate and logical result of a loss of trust is DISTRUST which accounts for the spectacular growth of the phenomenon we call 'fake news'. Nothing is taken at its face value, the criterion for judging truth evaporates. 35% of Republicans in America don't trust national news organizations such as CNN.

The next casualty of this loss of trust is democracy. What accounts for the deep political divide in the United States that now threatens its hitherto stable and respected democratic system if not the loss of truth and the subsequent loss of trust? This climate of collective distrust, fake news and the eroded foundations of truth, also favours the emergence of insane conspiracy theories. It's a diabolical spiral of madness. We are seeing conspiracy theories emerge with greater frequency and at increasing levels of derangement. It is sufficient for a certain number of people to embrace a blatant 'untruth', like the stolen election of 2020, for it to be taken up by millions of people (in defiance of all evidence) and become a political battle cry. The claim that some key US democrats constitute a sinister cabal of blood-sucking pedophiles operating out of the basement of a pizza parlour, a striking piece of sheer insanity, became viral and was at the root of the QAnon movement. These glaring dysfunctions, revealing of a deep sickness in the psyche and soul of America, have ominous implications for the prospects of this nation. By giving all this insanity a voice, a significant portion of the responsibility lies with the explosion of social media.

At this point I am obliged to mention Metaverse, the unwelcome offspring of social media that has taken the unreality of our technological lives to a whole different level. We now have the opportunity to "live within our illusions"as writer for *The Atlantic*, Megan Garber, stated. We have finally arrived at George Orwell's and Aldous Huxley's brave new world of 'immersive entertainment'. "We will become so distracted and dazed by our fictions that we will lose our sense of what is real. We will make our escapes so comprehensive that we cannot free ourselves from them. The result will be a populace that forgets how to think, how to empathize with one another, even how to govern or be governed," Megan Garber added.

In addition, our mentality is so enfeebled that everything now must have 'entertainment value'. In the past, there was a time to be entertained and there was a time to go about the serious business of life and it was never considered that one could be a possible substitute for the other. No longer. The two have meshed. In an example, I recently came across, the entertainment imperative reached a high point of absurdity when Turbo Tax, a tax filing service, announced to its clients that: "We've pulled together this year's best tax moments and created your own personalized tax story!" Can anything be more ridiculous? The old-fashioned version of life that some of us were brought up with has become so insufferable in the eyes of the digital generation as to be rejected in favour of whatever unreal version has entertainment value!

'All the world is a stage. And all the men and women merely players,' as Shakespeare once expressed metaphorically, is now no longer metaphor. It is life in the Metaverse.

Have we touched bottom or is there more of this insanity in the pipeline?

So, if the sacrifice of truth wasn't intentional at the outset, which is quite plausible, but the unintended consequences are severe, what were the circumstances that permitted this to happen before our very eyes without our being able to control it?

The reasons are many, as I have already discussed, but one of the more consequential factors was the advent of algorithms. Nobody but those specialized in the field had heard or understood the meaning of the word thirty years ago. Now it virtually controls our lives.

It is the backbone of AI. You can't click on an item of interest on Google without it following you on the side of your screen like an infection for weeks, if not months. In the simplest terms, whatever captures our attention will be intensified by many multitudes. Whether it is with respect to markets or an individual, an algorithmic search engine can work through trillions of gigabytes of data and identify your preferences within fractions of a second. In this way information or disinformation gets to its target at lightning speed and scale. It is also information of great financial value to all the platforms which is why we don't have to pay for their services. The information highway has been revolutionized by algorithms but not in a good way. Truth, again, was the first casualty.

Now the reason I said that the reach and consequences of social media were not properly known and anticipated at the outset was that no one could have foreseen the sheer scale that was achieved in a very short time. In fact, many had doubts about the original business model. The explosion in users combined with the growing amount of time spent on devices converted the digital advertising industry into a cash producing monster. Digital advertising now drives 63% of all ad revenue in the US with Facebook and google accounting for 54% of that number. What was also unanticipated was that the power to change mentalities and influence values inherent to this phenomenon would have such an effect on social cultures worldwide. Where these cultures have long-standing roots, in the more traditional societies, say, the worst effects have been resisted to some degree; where this isn't the case – in America, for example – the effects have been devastating. In this critical moment in human history when our civilization can pivot either way and a quantum leap in our ways of thinking and being is urgently required of us, social media has been and will continue to be a substantial obstacle.

The use of the internet and portable digital technology has brought about another set of unfortunate outcomes that must also be mentioned in this context. In the LGBTQ community self-identification has increased markedly in this period. According to Gallup, more than 20% of GenZ Americans (age 20+) identify as lesbian, gay, bisexual or transgender. This figure is several times higher than for any previous generation and SEVEN times higher than for the Baby Boomers. But the really concerning development is that the state of mental health in the LGBTQ community is dire and getting worse. According to the Center for Disease Control (CDC), "close to 70% of LGBTQ students experienced persistent feelings of sadness or hopelessness during the past year and more than 50% had poor mental health during the past 30 days. Almost 25% of LGBTQ teenagers attempted suicide in the past year."

There is some good news on the horizon, however. In the November 2021 issue of *The Atlantic*, Ian Bogost wrote an article announcing that: "The Age of Social

Media is Ending. It Should Never Have Begun. I faithfully transmit what he wrote. "It's over. Facebook is in decline. Twitter in chaos. Mark Zuckerberg's empire has lost billions of dollars in value and laid off 11,000 people… It has never felt more plausible that the age of social media might end and soon. Connectedness was never a terrible idea – the problem came from doing so all the time, as a lifestyle, an aspiration, an obsession." His prescription: "To win the soul of social life we must learn to muzzle it again. To speak less, to fewer people and less often – and for them to do the same to you. We cannot make social media good, because it is fundamentally bad, deep in its structure. All we can do is hope that it will wither away and play our small part in helping abandon it."

Another piece of good news is that Utah has become the first US state to require social media firms to get parental consent for children to use apps under 18. Utah Governor, Spencer Cox, announced: "We're no longer willing to let social media companies continue to harm the mental health of our youth." More states are considering doing the same.

However, it was Derek Thompson of *The Atlantic* who asked the most pertinent question of all.

"In the open expanse of the internet, we could have built any kind of world.

We built this one.

Why have we done this to ourselves?"

2
CAPITALISM. FRIEND OR FOE?

I am choosing to devote this chapter to examining the nature of capitalism in America. The case of the world's richest democracy is worth close attention because what takes place in the US tends to leak into other advanced industrial societies with a time lag. The nature of American capitalism and its consequences on society, however, is unique to its culture and the sheer size of the nation. It is also revealing of the dark side of the 'laissez-faire' variant of capitalism not adopted by other western societies but fiercely defended by most Americans though very few have a proper understanding of the 'socialism' practiced elsewhere.

As a system of economic organization capitalism has been unrivaled in its ability to create wealth. There is no argument about that. In a historic chart of economic growth, the advent of capitalism illustrates the classic hockey stick formation, flatlining for millennia then going vertical. In its 250 (or so) year history of capitalism, the world has changed beyond recognition. The abundant availability of fossil fuel has had much to do with this success story but without capitalism's capacity to underwrite industrial development we could never have achieved what we now have. Theoretically, the primary function of capitalism has been the efficient distribution of goods and services as determined by supply and demand in the context of 'markets.'

While in theory the interaction of market forces sounds fair and effective, in practice it doesn't always work that way; the overriding flaw in the system being human nature. The explanation is simple. Any social or economic mechanism that relies on self-interest as its fundamental driving force, the case with capitalism, is bound to be unjust if a counteracting mechanism designed to curb its excesses is absent. Human nature cannot be relied upon to do the right thing on its own and yet that's what 'laissez faire' capitalism proposes. Moral considerations shouldn't enter into it, its hardcore supporters would argue. Those who embrace that doctrine see life in terms of a minority of deserving 'winners' who have the talent and determination to come out on top and a majority of 'losers' who don't. It is a stark, merciless, zero-sum conception of life that has a following in America owing to the highly individualistic spirit of the nation (Ayn Rand being its philosophical matriarch). This is the case, curiously, even among the ranks of those who have no chance of winning!

Most mature political cultures have demonstrated an understanding of the situation by imposing measures to limit the scope of personal egoism and ensure a modicum of social justice. Societies where such methods have been applied successfully have traditionally been the most stable. This has been the case of the Scandinavian societies, namely, Sweden, Denmark Norway and Finland but all western societies are social democracies to one degree or another except for America. In defiance of the example set by other nations, America bucks the trend and is consequently the most unequal society of them all. Owing to the dread of 'communism' that is deeply embedded in the American psyche, the word 'socialism' resonates negatively at all socio-economic levels. As a result, Joseph Schumpeter's "gale of creative destruction", that he rightly attributed to the nature of capitalism, has become something of a hurricane in the US.

For a better understanding of why this is the case, we must go back a little in history.

America as the land of opportunity, did not become the Eldorado it once was (and still is for some) by accident. That reality was created by the drive and ambitions of the early settlers and pioneers, who due to the harsh conditions under which they lived, were obliged to adopt an 'each one for himself' vision of life. They took risks, worked hard and with much willpower carved out better lives for themselves. As a result, they believed fanatically in self-reliance. Since then, not much has changed fundamentally. It's also the reason why Americans will not give up their right to own a gun. In the early days they were on their own with no one around to defend them. They took their knocks stoically and didn't expect the government to help them out. Furthermore, America is a vast land that didn't lend itself to any form of centralized control. For those toiling away in their homesteads or opening up the country in the west, Washington was something of an abstraction.

As time went on the incentives to prosper in the bountiful 'new world' were such that America became the coveted land of opportunity to which millions of people immigrated, in order to improve their lot. Again, it wasn't easy for these waves of newcomers at first and they only had their wits, hard work and determination to depend on. The self-reliant loner, as portrayed in movies by John Wayne and Clint Eastwood, became the symbol of American strength and masculinity (and for many it still is). This set the tone of the American ethos going forward and almost certainly would have persisted if it wasn't for the intervention of an unforeseen natural event in the 1930's that would alter the course of America's political development and introduce the notion of government assistance for the first time.

A severe drought in the mid-west and the failure of the settlers to prevent wind-caused soil erosion turned the food producing prairies of America into a dustbowl. It was a catastrophe for farmers who were no longer able to grow food and 60% of the population of the region emigrated to urban areas. The combined effect of this event with a sharp economic downturn rapidly developed into the Great Depression, the harshest socio-economic event to hit an industrial nation in the 20th century. In response to the human suffering, President Franklin Roosevelt put together a number of measures to alleviate the plight of the displaced farmers and the poor, giving rise to the New Deal, the first comprehensive piece of social legislation in America. The Great Depression was long and hard, but the New Deal saved the day. A decade later, America's involvement in the Second World War obliged it to ramp up the industrial might of the nation, that, having been spared the destructive consequences of war on its own soil, rapidly became the wealthiest and most powerful nation in the world.

The postwar years were the glory days of America. A robust and productive middle-class grew in prosperity and became the envy of the world. uring the Eisenhower, Kennedy and Johnson administrations that WERE still being shaped by the pre-war social programs of FDR (tax rates during the Eisenhower/ Kennedy administrations reached 91% on the upper brackets) inequality was moderate and a single earner could provide a family with decent housing, healthcare and education.

By the time Jimmy Carter became President in 1976, storm clouds had begun to appear on the horizon of the American economy and inflation was raising its ugly head in the form of 'stagflation' (low output, high inflation) due, among other things, to OPEC and the first oil price shock. The first signs that a moral infection was brewing in the heart and soul of the nation was the reaction of the American people to the scarcity of gasoline in the late 1970's. The Greatest Generation who had been shaped by the First World War and the Great Depression and who embodied qualities such as personal responsibility, humility and the work ethic, rapidly devolved into the post-war Baby Boom Generation that was an early incarnation of the more entitled and egoistic cohort that were to emerge later. Unable and unwilling to put up with even a moderate degree of austerity in what Jimmy Carter called "the moral equivalent of war" they were ready to move on to what they believed were to be bigger and better things under Ronald Reagan. Carter's 1979 speech denouncing the materialism of America sealed his political fate.

Ronald Reagan was elected with much fanfare in a landslide victory in 1980 announcing that it was 'Morning in America,' with the promise of prosperity by means of tax cuts, deregulation and less government. He was true to his word. As a result, the mild moral infection diagnosed in the Carter years became a full-blown tumour of greed that was to develop with increasing virulence for the next forty years. The rich got richer rapidly and the poor became poorer just as fast while the middle-class shrank beyond recognition (The Economic Policy Institute revealed that while workers' wages had been flat since 1978 , CEO pay had increased almost 1000% by the second decade of this century). The Reagan years was also the era of the shameless shenanigans of the Gordon Gekko's of high finance so well portrayed by Oliver Stone in his film *Wall Street*. Lines such as: "Greed is good – greed clarifies, cuts through and captures the essence of the evolutionary spirit," – well caricatured the spirit of the time, giving Oliver Stone's creation much sociological value. Shocking as it seemed at the time, the movie was relatively tame by comparison with what was to come.

The party only really got underway after the turn of the century.

To make up for the loss of revenue occasioned by significantly lower tax revenues, the squeeze on everyone but the rich took place. Millions of middle-class careers and jobs vanished as did fixed private pensions and affordable healthcare. Large sums of money needed to be borrowed to afford a college education. With lobbying having increased a 1000% percent to become the most lucrative business in Washington, the enforcement of anti-monopoly laws would end, while hundreds of tax dodges became legal.

In 2020 tech companies spent $80 million a year on lobbying while oil and gas spent $113 million. Nobody spends that kind of money without a significant quid pro quo. These can often be very unjust. For example, Uber and Lyft spent $200 million to promote Proposition 22 in California to make sure that transportation and delivery companies are free of the obligation to offer healthcare and other benefits to their drivers. Private healthcare premiums are largely unaffordable in America at that level of income.

Wall Street, the real winner in this self-serving free-for-all, quadrupled its share of the nation's income by becoming an arena for unlimited avenues of speculation and personal enrichment. While producing nothing of value to society, the stock and commodity markets became rigged casinos for insiders. Big business and the ruling elite, not sufficiently satisfied with these spoils, managed to roll back all meaningful controls of their political contributions (incomprehensibly declared unconstitutional by the Supreme Court) allowing them to spend limitless funds to influence elections that by then had become largely a question of money.

To compound this accumulation of wealth at the top of society, technological innovation was churning out 'unicorns' by the dozens, some of which had grown in such spectacular fashion that a parallel (financial) power nexus took root, exemplified by the likes of Bill Gates, Elon Musk, Mark Zuckerberg and Jeff Bezos.

At the very moment that San Francisco and Silicon Valley became the hub of the greatest concentration of billionaires on the planet, the streets of San Francisco became congested, dangerous and disfigured with drug addicts, the mentally sick and the homeless, living on the streets, dying, defecating and injecting themselves in the saddest display of human degradation in modern times – a grotesque demonstration of the gaping divide between the haves and the have nots that had emerged in America.

To believe that this was restricted to America would be an error. Brexit had its origins in much the same sentiments as those of Trump supporters, a country divided by a prosperous South-East (particularly London) and neglected parts of the Midlands and the North. The situation was not as extreme as in the US by any means, but the underlying causes have much in common. On account of the service industries which were concentrated in London, particularly finance and insurance, London boasted an insolent level of prosperity compared with the rest of the country, creating socio-economic distortions that become divisive.

While London property prices soared to the sky stoked by Russian oligarchs, foreign tax dodgers, speculators and the wildly excessive rates of remuneration of the financial sector, the majority of the country struggled. Rates of poverty in Britain are high for a first world nation (its median income is lower than Slovenia's). Faced with this toxic brew, newly elected PM Liz Truss, in a moment of incomprehensible Reaganism, thought that the way forward for the U.K was to lower taxes on the rich. Given the economic condition of the U.K, a first-year student of economics would understand the folly of such a policy. A combination of public outcry and the immediate sanction of the bond markets made her tenure in office justifiably the shortest in British history. Unlike America, the pound sterling does not benefit from the privilege of being the reserve currency of the world. The Bank of England can't print money with abandon without severe and swift consequences and so an immediate about-turn was instituted by the new chancellor of the exchequer. The U.K may have dodged a bullet on that occasion but the longer-term problems it faces are far from being resolved.

As nothing in life is ultimately free, to finance America's bonanza for the rich, The Federal Reserve (central bank of America) was unable to rely on tax revenues to meet its outgoings on account of years of the system being successfully gamed by the ruling elite. Warren Buffet paid less taxes proportionally than his secretary and Donald Trump paying less in income tax (not proportionally but in absolute terms) than a household making $20,000 a year! The government had to resort to creating money from thin air by what is euphemistically named Quantitative Easing (QE).

In addition, for billionaires to pay less taxes proportionally than those in the lower rungs of the socio-economic ladder, the American tax code must be on their side.

This is certainly the case and after being subjected to years of highly focused lobbying, it generously provided the ruling elite a multitude of ways they can shelter, camouflage or simply avoid revealing the full extent of their income or capital gains - all legal, thanks to armies of tax advisors trained for the sole purpose of ferreting out the required loopholes. In the meantime, lower earners, working from paycheck to paycheck, have no way to benefit from the multitude of deductions, write offs or any other of the byzantine privileges embedded in the tax code, suffer a disproportionate tax burden. "A recent study estimates that collecting unpaid federal income taxes from the 1 percent – not raising their taxes, just putting an end to their tax evasion – would add $175 billion to the public purse – almost enough to lift everyone out of poverty altogether." wrote Matthew Desmond of Princeton University for *The New York Times* in March 2023.

In addition, consider the following anomaly.

Income gained from selling stock in a company is taxed at a lower rate than income gained from working at that business. In other words, wealth accumulated while a person sleeps is privileged over the earnings of a person who actually creates the wealth. There should be no surprise, therefore, to learn that the 10% of Americans who are in a financial position to benefit from these circumstances, own 90% of stocks. How much more flagrant can incongruities such as this be? As a result, the rift between a hapless working class or what's left of the middle-class and the parasitic and privileged 'rentiers' at the top never ceases to widen. But apparently there's nothing new here. The 19th century philosopher and economist, Frederic Bastiat, already recognized these tendencies when he stated: "When plunder has become a way of life for a group of people in society, they create for themselves a legal system that authorizes it and a moral code that glorifies it."

Plus ca change....

In the last forty years, by these and similar methods, America has brought about the greatest transfer of wealth in history from the middle, lower and working classes to the top tier of society at the cost of not only impoverishing a large swathe of its population but of compromising the integrity of its political system in order to do so. Analysis of voting patterns in Congress reveals that both Democratic and Republican lawmakers consistently vote for the interests of their more prosperous constituents with scant attention to the rest. Once a system has been crippled to serve the interest of a minority, when forced to adapt or die, it can only die as the mechanism for adaptation has already been destroyed. What will then happen when climate change puts its foot on the accelerator? That same minority will then discover that they have sold the crown jewels for a mess of pottage (the destroyed social fabric of the nation) that can't, at that point, be of any benefit to them or their children – a striking reminder, as though we need one, of how you can't trust human nature to do the right thing when people are free to do the wrong thing. Egoism knows only one way to be.

Soon after the French Revolution, in a letter of advice to the French National Assembly in 1791, Edmund Burke wrote the following: "Men are qualified for civil liberty in exact proportion to their disposition to put moral chains on their own appetites. Society cannot exist unless a controlling power upon will and appetite be placed somewhere, and the less of it there is within, the more there must be without. It is ordained in the eternal constitution of things, that men of intemperate minds cannot be free. Their passions forge their fetters.". The fundamental flaw in the system is that wisdom is not remotely compatible with capitalism, as we know it, or with the socio-political cultures it has created.

Another consequence of allowing the fox to live undisturbed among the hens is that the American national debt ballooned to its present eye-watering $ 32 trillion and the annual budget deficit at over $3 trillion. It's a collective modern-day version of Louis XIV's decision to use the entire wealth of France at the time to satisfy his illusions of grandeur in the building of Versailles – a folly that cost him his life – and one that now threatens the durability of the American experiment.

Some of the claims I have made here concerning the nature of capitalism have been given an academic 'imprimatur' by French economist Thomas Piketty in his definitive work *Capital in the Twenty-First Century* which explored several centuries worth of statistics to present the argument that capitalism inherently makes the rich richer (although he probably didn't need 753 pages to come to that conclusion or convince us!). He called it 'patrimonial capitalism' in which a privileged class get rich via passive investment and inheritance while everyone else falls behind. "To someone who has always been privileged, equality begins to look like oppression," observed historian Carol Anderson.

Professors Anne Case and Angus Deaton (both of Princeton University) defined the situation in America in very clear terms: "Robin Hood was said to have robbed the rich to benefit the poor. What is happening in America today is the reverse of Robin Hood, from poor to rich. Political protection is being used for personal enrichment, by stealing from the poor on behalf of the rich, a process known to economists as rent-seeking. Public purpose and the well-being of ordinary people are being subordinated to the private gain of the already well-off." There you have it. Most mature industrial societies have long understood that the dynamic of self-interest that underlies Piketty's conclusions must be tempered. Social legislation to try and 'level the playing field' has played its part in attenuating the worst effects. America's cosmetic attempts to do the same has been nothing but smoke and mirrors.

What I have just described is a mostly macro view of this secular transformation. When you begin to focus on the individual human aspects, the situation rapidly becomes tragic. 'Deaths of despair' are now treated by statisticians, politicians and sociologists as a new category of death in the same way as they might refer to cancer, diabetes or cardiac arrest. They estimate these deaths at over 80,000 or so a year which, again, hides the terrible circumstances that strike entire families making men and women in large numbers destroy themselves through drug use, alcohol, obesity, and sheer despair to the point of death. This is fully acknowledged and taking place openly in the richest country in the world. Monstrous and unconscionable are words too mild to describe the moral abyss that must exist in a society for such a thing to be tolerated. "Poverty is a tight knot of humiliation and agonies and its persistence in American life should shame us", wrote Matthew Desmond for *The New York Times*. I read a report the other day that claimed that Jeff Bezos could single-handedly eliminate homelessness in the US as well as substantially raise the salaries of 700,000 teachers in America with just a portion of his wealth. And that is one man – and he hasn't done it.

In a book such as this one where I am trying to pull together the various threads that can give the reader some idea of the combination of factors that can explain the paradox in the title of this book, the capitalist system degraded by egoism, would certainly be one. But let's bear in mind that capitalism is just a mechanism, a system. It has no heartbeat. What gives life, direction and a dynamic to this mechanism is us – we the people who participate in it, willingly or not. It is for this reason that each one of us must become aware of the true underlying nature of the problem, first, in order to make sure we are not unduly contributing to it and secondly, to know how to counter its worst abuses. In this regard, we should remain mindful of the words of John Stuart Mill: "The only thing necessary for the triumph of evil is that good men should do nothing."

But to get back to the tentacle-like ramifications of collective greed in America we have to look at the most significant and telling repercussion of all – the election of Donald J. Trump. The mystery of how a vulgar, boastful, inept, megalomaniac like Trump was elected to the presidency of the United States is directly related to this development and can be unveiled quite easily.

In fact, it is not really a mystery at all. The general absence in the United States of social programmes along European lines resulting from the gold rush of greed of the last 40 years, meant that there was nothing that could prevent the working class of America who had lost their jobs to Mexico through NAFTA (half the population of Detroit) and globalization (3.5 million to China) from gradually sinking into poverty or near poverty (one third of American live below a first world level of poverty). As we have seen, families who don't earn a living wage cannot educate their children, maintain their health, remain married or eke out a modicum of contentment from their lives, experience intense despair.

But it's not just a question of money: "Jobs are the basis for the rituals, customs, and routines of working-class life. It is the loss of meaning, of dignity, of pride, and of self-respect that comes with the loss of marriage and community that brings on despair, not just or primarily the loss of money," wrote Case and Deaton (authors of *Deaths of Despair and the Future of Capitalism*). It is a condemnation to third world poverty in a first world country that nobody seems to care about. *The New York Times* editorialist Nicholas Kristof and his wife Sheryl Dunn portrayed this descent into hell of his school friends from a small rural area in Oregon in his book *Tightrope*. There was not one of them who survived beyond 60 years of age.

This same sad story was being played out across America.

It is little wonder that the large segment of society who have seen their standard of living drop steadily from one decade to the next, while others have never had it so good, would rebel against the general negligence and indifference to their plight. What better way to express their anger and resentment than to choose a man like Donald Trump to champion their cause. He was the perfect fit. "Trump's underlying ludicrousness, his manifest lack of the intellectual capacity and emotional maturity to be president was part of what endeared him to his base. You fancy liberals think you're so smart. Well, we'll show you, by electing someone you consider a clown!", wrote Nobel Prize winning economist Paul Krugman. The spoilt scion of a rich real estate family who had hustled his way to riches and who for years filled the gossip columns of New York suddenly saw the ultimate opportunity to satisfy his limitless vanity by becoming President of the United States. The infantile antics of this champion narcissist, to which Americans were subjected for four long years, could be viewed as a source of amusement if it wasn't for the fact that he was elected to the highest office on the planet – a concern not just for Americans but for the rest of the world.

For the first time in American history a brash and uncouth imposter banished all competition on his path (former governor of Florida, Jeb Bush, former Ohio governor, John Kasich and other such worthy contenders fell over like bowling pins) by becoming a master of a debating technique known as 'Gish Galloping', an unstoppable torrent of lies, distortions, deflections and distractions that the RAND Corporation called a 'firehose of falsehood'. Whether Trump honed this skill wittingly is uncertain, but it turned out to be an unbeatable tactic. The Gish Gallopers entire strategy rests on exploiting 'Brandolini's Law' which states that 'the amount of energy needed to refute bullshit is an order of magnitude bigger than to produce it.' Trump has an unsurpassed mastery in this field.

Can the world's premier democracy sink any lower?

Trump, it should be clear, was never authentically concerned with the cause or needs of his followers. He was astute enough to know that he must continuously stir up their anger and resentment in order, in the first place, to access the White House and then afterwards to try and keep the top job. For this to happen: "A lot of white Americans who are really threatened, are willing to reject democratic norms because they see it as a way to protect their status", said Ashby Jardins, a political scientist at George Mason University. It was obvious from the start, that his followers, who rejoiced at all his shortcomings, scandals and gaffes, wanted nothing more than to de-stabilize the ruling establishment.

This they were able to do when Trump was elected President in 2016, to the amazement of everyone including himself. He then proceeded to deal a succession of humiliating blows to the image and standing of the United States by angering America's closest allies, cozying up to Vladimir Putin and declaring his love for Kim Jong-un – all of which did nothing but add to the fervent support of the MAGA crowd!

Peter Wehner, writer for *The Atlantic*, set out this concise summation: "Trump has no attachment to the Republican Party or, as best one can tell, to anything or anyone else. His malignant narcissism prevents that. Trump is an institutional arsonist, peddling conspiracy theories, spreading lies, sowing distrust. That's his skill and he's quite good at it."

That, however, is where the amusing part ends (if you can call it that) and the far darker consequences of that election begin. By perverting capitalism to their own ends and favouring the circumstances whereby a man like Trump acceded to the White House, the ruling elite had unwittingly made a colossal error. Trump's failings were very damaging to the image of America in the world. The January 6th insurrection then tarnished the credibility of its democracy but that was not the extent of it. Trump's ultimate aim was to roll back free and fair elections so as to become some modern-day version of 'Il Duce' in the hope of presiding over the American empire for the foreseeable future. Mercifully, it didn't work out that way. American democracy was an inconvenient detail on his path, but it was touch and go for a while. This saga, however, has not yet ended.

But what Trump did manage to do during his time in office that was even more consequential than his other antics, was to infect the Republican party (the oldest political party in America, the party of Abraham Lincoln) with his lack of principles such that hitherto respectable senators and members of congress traded every scrap of their former integrity to vow fealty to a man who questioned the election results of 2020 and encouraged his armed followers to storm the Capitol. But the fact that he was able to accomplish this without much difficulty would suggest that the rot at the heart of the party and America itself, had set in long before he came on the scene.

At that point, it became clear that the greed of the ruling elite, arising many years earlier, was causing the American experiment to unravel. Why do I say this? Because that experiment, high-minded and idealistic as it was at the outset, was only as good as the underlying moral substance that brought it into being. The Civil War would have destroyed America if it hadn't been for the rock-like moral stature of Abraham Lincoln. Once that fundamental pillar begins to crumble, and that is what we have been witnessing over the last few decades, then the entire edifice starts to collapse, brick by brick.

Scott Galloway describes the disintegration of the social fabric as follows: "Distrust and lack of connection have resulted in systems failures. Specifically, the central compact of any society has been broken in America. For the first time in our nation's history, thirty-year-olds are not doing as well as their parents at the same age. Young men are failing, while the old and rich weaponize tax and regulatory policy to protect their wealth and still the gale of creative destruction. We are not just lonely. We have no collective vision. We not only cannot see landfall but wouldn't recognize it. We are adrift. Adrift doesn't mean lost. But we can't course-correct or agree on a direction. We have the largest vessel with the most robust propulsion ever imagined, and we have registered staggering prosperity – but scant progress. We are divided, angry, and more of us feel disconnected."

In the 18th century Benjamin Rush, one of the signers of the Declaration of Independence, predicted that the new nation that had just gained its independence "would eventually fall apart in an orgy of selfishness."

That prediction has come true, I fear.

3
CIVILIZATION IN JEOPARDY

Civilizations have lifespans. They ebb and flow. All indications point to the fact that we are quite far along the declining arc of this process; the final phase being one of exceeding bio-physical limits (bringing on climate change and resource depletion), excessive complexity (setting off entropic forces in social as well as economic areas) and, finally, decadence (a moral collapse leaking into our lifestyles, culture and politics). Worryingly, there is a pattern to this process that has been repeated reliably in the collapse of past civilizations, suggesting that the possibility of circumventing it is limited.

It should as news to no one, except the most resolute deniers of reality, that the world's climate, resulting from the greenhouse effect of accumulated CO_2 in the atmosphere, is changing the conditions of life on the planet. If this was an isolated phenomenon, like the ozone gap, it could be remedied in an isolated fashion. The case of climate change is quite different. It involves every thread of our existence, which is to say, any effective measure to reduce CO_2 would involve the total revamping of our industrial civilization.

As the idea of change on the required scale is not only unacceptable but also inconceivable to most people, we tweak around the edges of the problem and will continue to do so until catastrophe FORCES change upon us. In the meantime, the world will continue to be ravaged by resource depletion, droughts, extreme air pollution and an exponential rise in natural disasters. Furthermore, this unprecedented challenge is closely intertwined with and exacerbates the other challenges on the path of a maturing civilization, namely, the fragile nature of its productive, economic and political systems creating a dangerous combination of factors that hang over our heads like the sword of Damocles.

Environmentalist, William Ophuls refers to the socio-political fallout as follows: "Like Gulliver, the civilization finds itself tied down by a multitude of vested interests – physical, social, economic, financial, political and psychological. Enmeshed in this legacy of the past, it cannot save itself. Even if the will to change existed, it would take prodigious effort and many decades to overcome this legacy, but the will is lacking. The civilization's elites may understand that the system is dysfunctional, but fundamental reform would require major sacrifice on their part, so they fight to preserve their privilege and power instead."

This increasingly familiar but tragic saga is being streamed before our eyes on a daily basis.

Owing to the implacable laws of thermodynamics, particularly the Second Law, all things in the universe are subject to entropy defined as diminishing returns as applied to energy. But as energy is involved in every human productive activity, it has repercussions on everything we do. Mature, complex civilizations such as ours pay a heavy entropic tribute for all their 'achievements'. This is not sufficiently acknowledged. I have described some of these blowback effects on our social, economic and political system in the Chapter 2 on capitalism, above, but they deserve further examination.

Take agriculture, for example. Virgin soil is a complex ecosystem containing a treasure trove of biological and chemical elements that are used in the production of food for human consumption. Modern farming methods, however, make no attempt to merge with the natural ecology of the soil but instead violate it in a multitude of inorganic ways (the heavy use of synthetic chemicals, for example) that are insensitive to its needs. The result is depletion of the vital elements in the soil (its fertility) inflicting long-term damage to its integrity and also causing erosion. It's not that better forms of farming don't exist, they do, but the use of methods for compensating for the loss of soil vitality such as crop rotation, manuring and so on are not deemed feasible given the quantity of food that is required to feed the planet – or so the argument goes.

The result is that a plate of food produced by industrial agriculture incurs the loss of TEN times as much energy as the plate contains. And so it is with virtually all forms of production when the energy coefficient is taken into consideration. Looking at it from this angle, we see that the infrastructure, size and complexity of modern society is literally eating up the planet. Although this may not be apparent to most westerners who continue to have an unlimited range of consumer products to choose from (that they believe will always be available) the damage is being done behind the scenes and the ecological noose that many choose to ignore, tightens by the day.

But warning signs are becoming increasingly hard to miss. Of these, water shortage is one of the most significant. 'The Law of the Minimum' dictates that the scarcest resource controls all the others and in this case, it is water. The situation with water is becoming critical and it can't be remedied except by natural means and nature is no longer on our side. It gives us too much or too little rain. Measures such as cutting down forests that moderate climate create rainfall and store water, could have been taken earlier, but now it's too late. The consequences have been implacable. Severe drought conditions have severely reduced crop yields in France in 2022. The same in the US, Brazil and other agricultural producers. Diminishing water tables, drying riverbeds and depleted reservoirs are threatening the future of California. A 23-year megadrought has left the southwest United States at its driest in 1200 years (based on tree-ring data). The effects of disappearing glaciers are being felt everywhere.

Now, an impartial onlooker would say, why did we not see the signs of danger and moderate our ways earlier before things got out of hand. Such a simple and reasonable question would seem to call for a simple and reasonable answer but that's not allowing for an important variable, namely, human nature, that embodies the most powerful of human instincts, egoism. As in the case of capitalism and virtually all human activity, this one inconvenient factor changes everything. It is of the nature of egoism to authorize the self (individually or collectively) to want more and more without thought for the consequences in the same way that an alcoholic who drinks has little concern for his health.

But here's the essential conundrum we are faced with. The urge for personal and collective 'more,' the driver of economic growth, has also been the cause of the spectacular material achievements that have taken place in the last two hundred and fifty years. Who would want to turn the clock back on that? If the world had been peopled by ascetics during that period, we would probably still be riding horses and using a hoe (as they still do in some parts of Cuba). The reason 'self-interest' (aka egoism) has become elevated to the ranks of a virtue in economic terms, is that it is generally acknowledged that it has spared us such a fate (endorsing Gordon Gekko's triumphant announcement that 'greed is good'). Self-interest is rightly identified as the engine of capitalism that has brought billions of people out of poverty. For all these reasons, the motivational drive born of egoism that is the sine qua non of success in business (or in life, for that matter) has become an unspoken mark of distinction.

At what point did this glaring moral contradiction cease to be one?

Listening to journalists on a financial channel like CNBC or Bloomberg is revealing of the process of 'normalization' in this regard. In the perfectly reasonable and matter-of-fact way financial journalists talk about money, they manage to turn vices (greed, selfishness in all its guises) into virtues (being competitive, assuming your financial responsibilities, being effective in business) while making constant appeals to our basest instincts. The result of this deft process, is that no one seems to notice that investment advice, which is what these channels peddle 24/7, has made the ways we manage our money 'respectable' and unquestioned. In this manner, we all, even the most well-intentioned and ethical among us, become invested in the sins of capitalism. How on earth can such a system be reversed?

From the point of view of an entire civilization it is important to look at the existing situation as you would a common balance sheet with its debit and credit columns. The entity we call 'Earth' is in the business of converting ecological wealth (the credit column) into economic prosperity (the debit column) for an ever-growing number of people. Carried along by the tidal wave of 'progress' we have witnessed over the last century little thought is given to the fact the credit and the debit columns become reversed. As ever-growing demand clashes with ever dwindling supply, we continue to draw down our ecological credit while increasing our debt to the planet. When that process is far gone, the case at present, efforts are then made to slow or prevent further drawdown, usually by technological means, to avoid the outcome that William Ophuls referred to earlier. This can sometimes buy time but nothing more. You can't reduce a debt once it is incurred except by paying it down and that is impossible in this instance. The result is that the debits grow indefinitely while the credits are exhausted which is what is meant when it is said that we have exceeded the 'carrying capacity' of the Earth.

William Ophuls sums up the situation as follows:

Civilization is trapped in a thermodynamic vicious circle from which escape is well-nigh impossible. The greater a civilization becomes, the more the citizens produce and consume – but the more they produce and consume the larger the increase in entropy. The longer economic development continues, the more depletion, decay, degradation, and disorder accumulates in the system as a whole, even if it brings a host of short-term benefits. Depending on a variety of factors – the quantity and quality of available resources, the degree of technological and managerial skill – the process can continue for some time but not indefinitely. At some point, just as in the ecological realm, a civilization exhausts its thermodynamic 'credit' and begins to implode.

Are we there yet?

To answer that question, we have to go back for a moment to the question of 'carrying capacity'. A wide range of repercussions arise from violating the inherent limits on growth that going beyond our 'carrying capacity' implies. Of these the most important and least obvious is that we have entered a secular period of stagnation. With an iPhone in everyone's hands and the talk being all about electric cars, space tourism, robots and 200-year life spans, it would seem churlish to claim that we are in a period of little progress and stagnation. But that is in fact the case.

Other than what has been created in and around cyberspace, the innovations of the last 50 years have been modest in comparison to the advent of the steamship, the railroad, mass production assembly lines, interstate highways, jet travel or high-speed trains in more recent times. It's only because we now take most of these accomplishments for granted that many people think that the recent wave of technological innovation has been an all-time gamechanger. The truth is that we live at a time of relative technological stagnation. The iPhone, social media and the multitude of Apps that exist have changed our lives far less than the transition from horse-drawn carriages to cars or being able to cross the Atlantic in 6 hours instead of 7 days or even central systems of heating and cooling our homes. Ask a resident of Florida if he or she would prefer an electric car to air conditioning. It's also worth remembering that we went to the moon, not last year or the year before, but 53 years ago!

"For much of the 19th and 20th centuries almost every generation of Americans was more productive, wealthier and longer lived than the one before it. In the past few decades, progress has faltered – and faith in it has curdled. Technological progress has stagnated, especially in the non-virtual world. So have real incomes. Life expectancy has been falling in recent years," tells us Derek Thompson of *The Atlantic*.

A group of Stanford University economists produced a paper to pose the question: "Are Ideas Getting Harder to Find." Their reply: "We present a wide range of evidence from various industries, products, and firms showing that research effort is rising substantially while research productivity is declining sharply." Pentagon researcher Jonathen Huebner created a model-tracing innovations for the last six hundred years of western history revealing a slow ascent followed by a rapid descent. In response to Huebner, *New York Times* editorialist, Ross Douthat writes: "To Huebner, this rise and fall pattern implies that we are reaching some inherent limit on possible innovation; indeed, he boldly suggests that we are around 85 percent of that limit, that we'll hit 95 percent by the late 2030's and then approach 100 percent thereafter."

If that is indeed the case, in one important sense, we have entered a period unlike any other in history. Periods of decline in the past were followed by periods of renewal in much the same way that a forest burned to ashes will consequently sprout with increased vigour. I suspect that the reason this time is different is that at no time in the past had we reached the finite LIMITS to growth (surpassing the planet's carrying capacity) from depleted or abused resources or were facing the accumulated entropic fallout from unbridled economic development in general. To this, we must add the impact of climate change that is every bit as consequential, but which together increase the effects by several multiples.

There is also a significant psychological impact. The world has become a roulette wheel of climate disaster that has us all on edge. What if that flash flood that destroyed houses in the next town came to your village next? What if that hailstorm that demolished your neighbour's roof had hit yours? What if the terrible hurricane of 2022 (the worst on record) that devastated parts of the west coast of Florida were to hit the east coast where you live in 2023? How does a nation recover from an earthquake like the recent one in Turkey? - and so on. It is hard to be sanguine about the future when it may be taken away from you at any moment.

Taking all this into account, a better sense of why the present conditions on the planet can be viewed as 'the worst of times' comes into focus along with the recognition that a perverse synergy exists between good and bad times, one being the cause of the other. Also, what we have lost by having gained so much is a reduced landscape of possibilities. By comparison with earlier times, the material world seems picked over, which is why most of the progress we now see is in cyberspace. Experiencing the energy and boldness that comes with opening new physical frontiers is no longer a reality (the world was thoroughly explored and mapped out a long time ago).

Most paths are well-trodden, and we are not about to re-invent the wheel. Furthermore, there seems to be less interest or scope for discovering philosophic, artistic and intellectual 'new worlds' – except in perfectly absurd ways. Political theories – democracy, communism, fascism, authoritarianism and every shade in between – have all been tried. Spirituality, the only dimension of life that remains largely unexplored is misunderstood or overlooked by the majority of mankind. As a result, a discomforting sense of end-of-history prevails, particularly among the young. The claims of politicians that 'better times' are around the corner ring strangely hollow in this context. No one believes them anymore. Conviction is lacking and we have arrived at an exhaustion of hope.

What happens when a guiding ideal is lost?

'Liquid modernity' are the words used by the Anglo-Polish sociologist, Zygmunt Bauman, to describe a condition of society in its twilight phase that is shallow, fluid and lacking in foundation. It is perceived as open, free and dynamic, but has no clear sense of direction. You see symptoms of this condition in most modern societies who have distanced themselves from their traditional roots. America, of course, being a pioneer in this respect. Liquid modernity stands for the promise of technological innovation and digital interconnectedness, financialization, the globalization of business and commerce and the opportunity (for some) of rapid wealth accumulation by these means. In this context, traditional skills, craftmanship, commitment to quality, pride and satisfaction in a 'job well done', a life perhaps modest in material riches but rich in fulfilment, are viewed as outdated, irrelevant and constricting and more suited to 'developing' nations than a modern society.

In this high-speed, ever-evolving digital world where people are free to 're-invent' themselves as they adapt to the requirements of the moment, such an 'old-school' vision has no resonance. The gig economy is built on this new perspective. The problem is that this concept, as so much in the modern world, is illusory. It's not founded on anything solid and sustainable. The style of life people are obliged to adopt in these circumstances is weightless, has no meaning, is spiritually void and sets their inner lives adrift. Success or failure is not just financial it is: "failure to make one's life cohere, failure to realize something precious in oneself,", we are told by sociologist Richard Sennett.

Referring to the liquid modernity of America, social historian Morris Berman stated:

> The irony for Americans is that in the fullness of time, the limitless possibilities and the absolute weightlessness of choice become as suffocating as the social restrictions of the past. Americans cannot choose NOT to participate in the utterly fluid, high-pressure society that the United States has become. Liquid modernity is, in short, quite rigid, a world of compulsive self-determination. But since it is norms that make life possible,

when normlessness becomes the norm, the social order becomes a hall of mirrors. This way of life may prove to be the greatest discontinuity in human history.

When civilizations 'peak', characterized by this form of discontinuity, which is arguably where we stand now and have been for a while, things can turn from sweet to sour very quickly which is why that pinnacle seems to incorporate both elements. The weakened grip on reality and the resulting moral exhaustion that characterizes such a moment in time, could also explain why today's pioneers have become a group of techno-visionaries with manic plans to colonize space or use bio-engineering methods to transcend humanity itself.

William Ophuls has somber words to describe the declining arc of civilization:

> Frivolity, hedonism, cynicism, pessimism, narcissism, consumerism, materialism, nihilism, fatalism, fanaticism - suffuse society. Politics is increasingly corrupt, life increasingly unjust. A cabal of insiders accrues wealth and power at the expense of the citizenry, fostering a fatal opposition between haves and have-nots. Mental and physical illness proliferate. The majority worships celebrities instead of divinities, taking its bearings from below rather than above.

This undeniable snapshot of our time is further reflected in the following statement by the distinguished historian Jacques Barzun: "The forms of art as of life seem exhausted; the stages of development have been run through. Institutions function painfully. Repetition and frustration are the intolerable result."

As early as 1922, in his landmark masterpiece *The Decline of the West*, German historian-philosopher, Oswald Spengler, already considered that civilization was in permanent and irretrievable decline.

At the core of the problem of modern societies reaching their limits in this way is that a zeitgeist such as 'liquid modernity' along with the inhuman scale of the infrastructure that exists, engenders an immense inner emptiness. This state of confusion as to ends and means is filled with superficial and trivial activities (see Chapter 2) and a marked lack of moral and spiritual sustenance. But this inner void is not without consequence. The inner emptiness that this condition fails to address leads to psychological problems, that range from multiple forms of neurosis to full-blown mental derangement. Examples abound.

It is November 2022 as I write and there have already been 606 mass shootings in America this year, an absolutely dismaying statistic that defies a simple explanation. A study by *Just Facts* examining murders in 2021 based on death certificate data project that, if the murder rate remains constant, one out of 179

Americans will eventually be murdered over the course of their lifetime. 100,000 people a year are dying from drug overdoses. According to a study published in *Lancet Regional Health*, depression in people 18 and older leaped from 8.5% in 2019 to 28% in 2020, then to an astounding 33% in 2021. Other studies reveal that 54% of Americans suffer from some form or degree of mental illness. The grim data on psychopathology in America points to a psycho/spiritual collapse of an unprecedented order. The cauldron of human suffering that underlies such data is unimaginable.

David Brooks, editorialist for *The New York Times* wrote an article using statistics that David Rozado, Ruth Hughes and James Halberstadt had assembled from analyzing 23 million headlines published between 2000 and 2019 by 47 news outlets. The results reveal that media headlines grew significantly more negative during that period with a greater proportion showing a preponderance of emotions such as anxiety, fear, disgust and sadness (corresponding to Scott Galway's conclusions about the effects social media). How does this data correlate with the general state of American mental health? The General Social Survey that rates levels of happiness reveal that between 1990-2018 the share of Americans who put themselves in the lowest category of happiness increased by more than 50%.

Now, one might be tempted to think that these statistics are confined to the very particular conditions existing in America and would not necessarily apply to the rest of the world. Unfortunately, that is not the case. Gallup surveyed roughly 150,000 people in 140 countries, including countries such as India, China, Brazil and Mexico, with reference to their emotional state. Negative emotions relating to stress, sadness, anger and physical pain hit a record high last year.

Again, when trying to thread the needle of the great paradox of our time, we need to examine a variety of social and economic developments to get a more complete picture of the situation. Take a single metric like marriage – rates of marriage have been declining precipitously since 1980. With what effect? Research shows that fewer marriages lead to less economic activity, less happiness, more loneliness, depression, crime and suicide. Furthermore, a growing number of single, under-educated, under-employed or unemployed, bored, lonely and depressed young men: "Is a malevolent force in any society, but it's a truly terrifying one in a society addicted to social media and awash in coarseness and guns", stated Scott Galloway. In fact, referring to the numbers, it is far more deadly than domestic or international terrorism. "Young men now have a greater chance to be killed by fire arms in the US than American soldiers serving during the Afghanistan or Iraq wars.", according to Joel Kotkin of Chapman University.

In 2022 there have been two mass shooting (4 or

more people dead) EVERY DAY on average in the US with no less than 40 school shootings from the beginning of the year until November. They reached their peak in mid-July when the US witnessed 15 mass shootings over a single weekend, according to *Gun Violence Archive* data. These shootings in 2023 outpace those of 2022 with 82 mass shootings so far (it is February) up over 25%. All this has become tragically routine in the US. The death of the shooter in these instances has become a recognized form of suicide (suicide by cop, it is called) the act of an empty, angry, lonely person whose heart and soul has been destroyed and who no longer wishes to live – and there are more and more of them. The 15-year-old who is accused of killing four students at his high-school in Oxford, Michigan in 2021 wrote the following in his journal: "The first victim has to be a pretty girl with a future so she can suffer like me."

It is with some reluctance that I have to refer to these terrible events, but I do so only to bring home the fact that every effect has a cause and a society can't brush under the carpet the essential needs of a significant section of its population without creating fertile terrain for such tragedy. It also demonstrates something I referred to earlier. The core values of a nation cannot be based on materialism alone. Traditions long in the making cannot be waived at will. All that is precious in life cannot be sacrificed at the altar of business and commerce in the context of a merciless economic system without extinguishing the soul. Why else would such a large number of seemingly 'ordinary' people living seemingly 'normal' lives destroy each other for no reason if their humanity had not been eclipsed by the de-spiritualized condition of their lives.

And it is at this point that I have to include the most shameful and telling statistic of them all; one that reveals the true nature of this slow-motion tragedy – and it not just in the US but worldwide. Gallup announced that the top 20 percent of the world is experiencing the HIGHEST level of happiness and well-being since Gallup began measuring these things while the bottom 20 percent is experiencing the WORST.

4

FINANCE.
THE DAY OF RECKONING
APPROACHES

The ticking time bomb threatening our civilization, while not as cataclysmic as a nuclear conflagration, but far more probable, is the fragile condition of the financial world. I briefly touched on this in the prior chapter on capitalism, but it bears looking into more closely. In the simplest terms possible, we have been living beyond our means for a very long time, with the result that the world is awash in unrepayable debt. Except on paper, money has become divorced from all real value which is why you need more and more of it to buy the same amount of goods.

Swiss financier, Egon von Greyerz estimates that the market for derivatives stands at $2 Quadrillion (an unfathomable number to most people including myself) that he believes to be far too conservative. On top of that you have $300 trillion in regular debt as well as several additional hundreds of trillions in unfunded liabilities for a grand total of $2.5 Quadrillion. In the meantime, global GDP stands at a mere $80 Trillion. What this means is that this gargantuan mountain of debt has little correspondence to the total of all goods and services produced in the global economy and therefore no longer has any real value. It is all synthetic. It is like tipping an Olympic swimming pool into a bathtub, the excess water being the inflationary impact. It is little wonder that in terms of gold, which has been the traditional method of how tangible value is measured over time, all the fiat currencies in the world have lost from 95-99% of their value since 1971.

So, what exactly are these dangerous instruments we call 'derivatives?' As with so many things in the arcane world of finance, different names are given to the same thing so that the perception of what it is can vary. This is not unintentional. Derivatives are debt that doesn't show up on balance sheets. They are 'off the books', so to speak, which permits over-indebted institutions to present a misleading semblance of financial health.

However, the moment the debt/derivative bubble bursts (which is what happened in 2008) it all becomes one and the same and the huge volume of illusory wealth that has been created will pop, with it dragging down all asset classes whose supposed worth was merely a function of wildly inflated values. There is nothing abstract or theoretical about any of this. The repercussions are very real indeed. Take the recent case in the United Kingdom. After the delirious 'mini-budget' proposition of the 'now you see her, now you don't' Prime Minister, Liz Truss, pension fund pressure was such that the Bank of England was forced to intervene with a 65 billion pound bailout, the UK pension funds having resorted to the derivatives market for liquidity. The implications are frightening. Pensions, one needs hardly to be reminded, keeps elderly people who are no longer in the work force, alive. It's very concerning (and a sign of desperation) that the British government tacked so close to the wind on this issue. Now that interest rates are being increased to fight inflation, the economy will likely enter into a prolonged period of low growth or recession.

One of the most successful hedge fund managers in the world, John Singer of Elliott Management, who is not in the business of frightening off his investors, has come out and said that they cannot assume that they had 'seen everything' because they survived the dot.com crash or the Great Recession. The world is on the path to hyperinflation, he contends. The extraordinary period of cheap (read, free) money is coming to an end and has "made possible a set of outcomes that would be at or beyond the boundaries of the entire post-Second World War period."

Switzerland, the bastion of conservative financial rectitude in the past, where your money was as safe as gold, also got caught up in American-style financial shenanigans. The previously venerable Credit Suisse got into trouble with 'dollar swaps' (another term for derivatives) that occasioned a run on the bank, inconceivable in the past. This reached a head in March 2023 when there was a forced takeover of CS by UBS (Union des Banques Suisse). These desperate, last-minute measures are nothing more than 're-arranging the deck chairs on the *Titanic* making the endemic problems larger rather than smaller. The Swiss National Bank, that oversees the most speculative hedge fund in the world, lost 142 billion Swiss francs, as much as its capital and the equivalent of the entire Swiss GDP. In fact, the Swiss banking sector as a whole represents five times Swiss GDP. All of these banks were among the safest in the world until they joined the ranks of US casino banking. In Germany, Deutsch Bank, a giant in the field and a well-established rogue of international finance, has flirted with collapse several times, but as it falls into the privileged category of being 'too big to fail' it will be bailed out until there's not enough money in heaven to do so.

So, to weave these facts into our central theme, the sharp pivot in America in the 1980's towards a laissez faire bonanza for the rich, decades later, not only destroyed the fabric of its own society but infected the entire world with financial instability. Debt has always existed. After all, the traditional business of banks was to take in deposits and to lend money for business development. In measured doses this accelerates the productive growth of an economy. In excess, on the other hand, it threatens the entire system. The orderly transfer of wealth to the rich known as the Reagan 'supply side revolution' was very costly to the United States government. The machine of the State must be financed somehow and running up the national debt was the only way.

By the time the Great Recession happened it was far too late to balance the books. Any attempt to do so would have precipitated the second Great Depression or worse, so that option was off the table. The era of Quantitative Easing (QE), the euphemistic term used by central banks to keep interest rates artificially low by buying its own debt, came into its own as never before. But let's be clear, QE is money created out of nowhere. By failing to raise revenue in a more traditional manner, the Federal Reserve had no option but to resort to such methods, however. It was obliged to bail out the perpetrators of the sub-prime mortgage debacle (the biggest swindle in modern times) or the economy would have collapsed overnight. But it didn't stop there. It continued to subsidize corporate America with its policies of easy money and zero interest rates ever since. This placed America and the rest of the world on a slippery slope of uncontrollable debt creation, corporate dependence on low rates of interest and a sudden reversal of course would have led to disaster. The sizeable pandemic bailout that ensued some years later, wholly justified in this instance, only served to aggravate the situation.

To sum it up. Since 1971, total debt in the US went up a dismaying 50 times!

The beneficiaries of this financial crime, as we have discussed earlier, are the wealthy in the top tier of society. Knowing full well that all this money in the bank is losing value by the day, they proceeded to buy hard assets like real estate, the value of which has become so inflated that an ever-larger number of people can't afford it. It is not uncommon for those in that category to own four or five homes, some of them unused. But even for them it doesn't ultimately make sense. It will be like "winning at poker on the *Titanic*," as the late financier Jimmy Goldsmith once said. The reason, he said, is because there isn't the slightest possibility that this debt can ever be repaid or reduced. In fact, even the interest can't be paid except by taking on further debt. It's a Ponzi scheme of gigantic proportions and we will all have to pay the piper eventually, not in money – it would have lost its value by then – but in human suffering. Nobody knows when that will happen. Central banks have been able to 'kick the can down the road' with some skill so far. This will continue for some indeterminate amount of time but not indefinitely: "Civilizations behave like all complex adaptive systems. They function in apparent equilibrium for some unknowable period. And then, quite abruptly, they collapse. The shift from consummation to destruction and then to desolation is not cyclical. IT IS SUDDEN," said historian Niall Ferguson.

In the meantime, how the gap between 'good times' and 'bad times' is perceived depends entirely, as the earlier Gallup survey suggests, on your financial standing. If you find yourself ambling down Bond Street in London, Avenue Montaigne in Paris or the Bahnhofstrasse in Zurich you can be forgiven for thinking that all is well in the best of all possible worlds (particularly if you don't read the news). In an atmosphere of blissful insouciance, people pop in and out of shops that showcase some of the most expensive merchandise in the world (LVMH the French luxury goods conglomerate has just announced record profits for the year) where a belt, scarf or handbag can cost thousands of pounds. From my own personal experience, I have noticed that, by and large, those in that category don't actually KNOW what is happening on the other side of the divide. It won't come naturally to their attention unless they make it their business to do so, and few do. As a result, they live in an impenetrable bubble and don't really wish to be reminded of conditions outside. In fact, in a social context, it would be considered an inexcusable 'faux pas' to even broach the subject!

This was the situation in the US prior to the election of Donald Trump. The top quintile of America, comprising the intelligentsia, the upper middle class and the ruling elite who run the show, openly admitted after Trump's stunning election victory in 2016, that they were caught off guard, couldn't see it coming and had little idea of how the other half, his electoral base, actually lived. As I wrote in my book *Time Is Running Out*: "The fact is, that if you are a well-off, educated and bi-coastal American, there is little reason to ever brush with that other half. Your entire universe is separated from them to the point where, in anything but an anecdotal sense, they don't exist."

The very same thing applies to climate change. The level of denial, particularly by those who believe they will be spared the worst of its consequences (a delusional notion, in itself), is very similar. Climate calamity and the danger of financial catastrophe are running neck and neck in terms of the threat they represent to the survival of our civilization. As a result, denial of these twin realities remains ferocious, indicating that certain people are willing to pull the wool over their own eyes in order to preserve the illusion that they live in the 'best of times' for as long as it lasts. Others who do not have that luxury have little doubt that they are living in 'the worst of times'.

No attempt to unravel the causes of this paradox would be complete without a discussion on education. After all, the social and political stability, as well as the overall functioning of a society, is only as good or effective as the quality of its education (in the widest sense) enjoyed by most of its citizens. It is the foundation on which the entire edifice rests. Underpinning this socio-cultural edifice is the collective 'sensibility' of a nation. Although hard to define in precise terms, sensibility is a distillation of traditionally transmitted values absorbed from the earliest moments of life as well as the instincts and emotions that develop subsequently that are conditioned by these values. The overall culture of a society is the cumulative expression of this process. It is also the unique source of the 'identity' of its people. A weak sensibility translates into a shallow culture, a fragile identity and varying degrees of personal insecurity. We must know and sense the strength and depth of our roots.

A society that breaks with the organic process that favours the natural development of sensibility and tries to re-invent itself in the image of what it considers a more 'modern' and pragmatic conception of how things should be is playing with fire. A typical example would be the adoption of novel and untraditional methods of child education. Time-tested methods of parental childcare and nurture are foundational when it comes to the development of sensibility. It is a highly risky endeavour for self-designated 'experts' to suddenly decide to break with tradition and institute better methods of doing this. It is for this reason that traditional European societies, such as France, Italy, Greece or Spain, not only have very distinct sensibilities but very secure identities also. They benefit from an underlying MORAL CONSENSUS that French sociologist Emile

Durkheim referred to as the 'conscience collective', an interaction of commonly held beliefs and sentiments that ensures social coherence and acts as a social glue. To one degree or another, this has been the case with most western industrial societies until now, but we are starting to see troubling signs that this essential consensus is breaking down.

Here again, the prime example in the West of a disappearing moral consensus, a weakened sensibility and a resulting deep socio-political divide, is the United States – as disunited as any time since the Civil War. Concurrent with this development are declining educational standards, an increasingly trivial and hollowed-out culture and a strong identification with jingoistic beliefs in America's economic and military supremacy or illusory ones such as the 'American Dream' to compensate for the absence of a sustaining foundation to their lives. Free of the cohesive forces of tradition and a 'conscience collective', a nation rapidly becomes 'unglued', which is to say, vulnerable to divisive internal (and external) demons. This is exactly what we witness today in the US.

The extremes of inequality we see in America today are not only socio-economic but educational. It has some of the best schools and universities in the world, but it also has the worst. Certain sectors of society reveal dismaying levels of under-education but taken as a whole, educational levels tend to be sub-par with little awareness or understanding among a sizeable portion of the population of what is going on in the world beyond its own borders. In one study I came across it was estimated that over 100 million Americans are functionally illiterate (can read but are unable to understand the real meaning of the words they read) a figure that is hardly credible until you learn that a significant number of people can't find the US on a world map, believe they can take a train to Hawaii, make contact with aliens or who don't know who the enemy was in the Second World War. Even if it was half that number, this level of ignorance is inexcusable in the richest country in the world. However, the relevance of all this becomes clear with the political repercussions of a large number of insufficiently educated people – some of whom are unable to distinguish a simple truth from a lie – voting in elections.

How did the richest democracy in the world get to this point? A clue.

What happens when most of a nation's money is being siphoned off into the hands of a tiny minority of its people who contribute insufficient amounts to the national treasury? Answer: there isn't enough left over for the important things that a government should provide for its citizens, of which the quality of school teachers is arguably one of the most vital of all (along with healthcare).

The following information and comments coming from US Education Secretary Miguel Cardona tells us part of the story: "Teachers are having to have two or three jobs in order to make ends meet. As a result, 53% of public schools reported being understaffed at the beginning of the 2022-23 year". A National Education Association survey released in January revealed that 55% of teachers say they will leave teaching earlier than planned. Both a lack of pay and a perceived lack of respect have contributed to teacher shortage. The consequences, however, are far reaching: "When schools shut down, the community shuts down," Cardona remarked. Teachers (inflation adjusted) wages have been mostly flat since 1996, while wages of other college educated graduates went up 30%. Most tellingly, a study published in 2019 in *Education Next* shows that improved conditions for teachers directly impacts student performance.

The nurturing of the human mind and spirit on which the moral and psychological health of a society depends, is the primary responsibility first of a parent, then a teacher but also a government. It is the latter that enables the former to complete their task under the most favourable conditions. What is the point of spending $900 billion on military defence if vital interests such as the proper education of a large part of the citizenry are consistently overlooked. Shouldn't those interests warrant some defense also? Shouldn't America be on a war footing to raise educational standards so as to provide an opportunity for all its citizens to improve their lives and that of the nation as a whole?

The fact that private schools and Ivy League Universities have excellent (and well-paid) teachers but cost hundreds of thousands of dollars to attend, only makes matters worse. Is there any wonder why this nation has never been as divided as it is now. An iron curtain of social and cultural differences but also of mutual incomprehension, has descended on this society that will be exceedingly hard to do away with. People from opposite sides of the divide might as well be from altogether different countries. Communication is difficult, the animosity is intense, there is no mutual trust and political or social bi-partisanship a thing of the past. Again, who or what is America defending when it spends five times more than any other country on defence but is at war within itself?

5

SPIRITUALITY. AN UNEVEN TRAJECTORY

Many years ago, in the City of London, one of the financial capitals of the world, there existed a code of honour that stipulated that "a gentleman's word was his bond". At the time, it meant that multi-million dollar contracts were sealed by a handshake. My first job after leaving university was in one of the oldest institutions in the City and I can attest to the fact that even if it wasn't literally a handshake, trust prevailed and for good reason; honour and integrity was alive and well. The world of business and finance had yet to be infected with toxic greed and immorality. My own father, the managing director (CEO) of a major oil refining and shipping company belonged to that generation. Greed was the last thing I would associate with him or with one of his closest friends, the Chairman of Shell, a very prominent businessman in the United Kingdom. at the time. Both were comfortably off, but neither was 'rich' in the meaning of that word today. Stock options, golden handshakes and multi-million-pound bonuses did not exist. Post-war taxes were very high. They were both content with what they had and felt privileged and fortunate to have it and were not reaching out for more. There was no great merit attached to any of this because those qualities were shared by most people at the time.

At the preparatory school I attended, the English teacher, a man of uncommon talent and intelligence, devoted his life to teaching 8–13-year-olds in a small school on the outskirts of London. His dedication to this task was such that he produced musicals at the school that he had written and composed himself, organized play reading sessions, constituted a fine library for the school and would read from a great classic novel in the last ten minutes of class to stimulate an interest in literature among his pupils. He was in his fifties, taught in a school that had no more than eighty boys, earned a modest salary, no doubt, but took to heart his responsibility to impart a higher vision of life to young boys, the importance of which they would only understand many years after he was gone – a very fine human being who was contented to live in obscurity in the service of others – an unsung hero in the true sense of the word. My debt to him is immense.

My final example is that of John Profumo, who was Secretary of State for War in the United Kingdom during the Harold Macmillan administration in 1960. His illicit relationship with Christine Keeler, a model who had also had a liaison with an attaché to the Russian embassy, that he at first denied in Parliament, but later admitted to, was a huge scandal in Britain at the time. Disgraced, he resigned his office in 1963 at the age of 48. For the rest of his life, this otherwise honourable man sought redemption working as a volunteer at a charity in East London (for which he was later rewarded with a CBE by the Queen). I ask myself, who would do such a thing nowadays? Do people even understand what the words 'atonement', 'penitence' or 'redemption' mean?

I cite these examples for one very important reason. To my mind, they all demonstrate moral/spiritual qualities at work in normal life. Not the spirituality of Zen masters and Hindu mystics, of course, but spirituality all the same. All human behaviour that arises from moral principles that are carried out with humility, kindness, consideration for others and a sense of duty or service to a larger good, is spiritual in my books. None of the people I mentioned believed themselves to be 'spiritual' or gave the notion a passing thought. Certainly not my father, the example I know best. For a long time, I didn't give him credit for the qualities he had because I was too busy ascribing to myself qualities I didn't have. A sage once said that 'spirituality begins with opening a door for an older person' suggesting that the range of spiritual behaviour begins with ordinary gestures of care and consideration for others. There are many rungs on that ladder, but the ones below are as important as the ones above.

The temptation of those who have had a deeper introduction to spiritual experience, might be to overlook the value and significance of those humble gestures as they grapple with more profound spiritual truths. I have no doubt been guilty of this myself. But if the word spiritual is to have any meaning in a Christian world it must be rooted in the example and teaching of Jesus Christ. Humility, Love and Compassion (or in more mundane terms – modesty, care, respect and consideration for others) are the fundaments of Christ's message as it applies to ordinary people in ordinary life – and those qualities are far more commonplace than we might think and every bit as worthy as other forms of spiritual practice. John Profumo may not have been a believer, possibly even an atheist, yet his humble struggle for atonement over many, many years in reaction to what today would be considered a passing 'peccadillo', demonstrated Christian qualities of a rare nature. It is worth remembering that Jesus, the humblest of the humble, cared only for ordinary people living ordinary lives. He was wary of the 'righteous'.

You could say that the immediate post-war period that I refer to was characterized by a form of 'innocence' compared to what was to come later. If that is so, the reason would be that certain essential Christian qualities were embedded NATURALLY in a certain way of life at the time (wonderfully portrayed in the British TV series 'Call the Midwife'). No one claimed those qualities for themselves because they weren't self-consciously aware of possessing them. Taoism in ancient China was based on the idea that the Tao (the universal principle of all life) works through people in such an organic manner that they are not aware of its manifestation within themselves. From a Taoist perspective, as soon as a person becomes conscious of his or her merit, the Tao is violated, and the value of that merit is compromised. The Sufi notion that 'a saint is someone who doesn't know he's a saint', is a similar idea. The nature of innocence, therefore, has a Taoist quality to it. The true spiritual practitioners of that time were not trumpeting their wisdom from the rooftops. Very few were known or were interested in being known. Taoist in spirit, they were living authentically spiritual lives. Some were also great teachers if you could find them. All this was to change dramatically over the next twenty years.

Fast forward a decade or two and spirituality had become fashionable. The baby boom generation, of which I am an early member, embraced the concept of spirituality with great enthusiasm. By the 1960's and 70's, spirituality had come out of the shadows and was 'au gout du jour'. Much was written on the subject. Many viewed it as a 'cool' and more evolved way to look at life and jumped on the bandwagon, often with a very superficial conception of what it was.

What had previously been the domain of a discreet minority suddenly became a mainstream movement with millions of followers. Outward signs of being a 'free spirit' (such as having long hair and wearing unconventional clothes) made its appearance conveying an image that also had some vague and indefinable association with spirituality. In a word, spirituality had become 'hip' and if you were 'square' you weren't moving with your time – the first troubling sign that the 'image' of something was gaining in importance over its substance.

In no time at all, self-appointed 'gurus' peddling every conceivable concoction of spirituality came out of the woodwork in large quantities. You couldn't enter a health food store anywhere without coming across a notice board with notes or cards announcing meditation sessions, Yoga, Tai Chi or workshops, conferences or teachings on Hinduism, Zen, Taoism, Sufism etc., a veritable cornucopia of spiritual possibilities. Bookstores had entire sections devoted to Mind, Body and Spirit literature as well as spiritual classics such as the Bhagavad-Gita or the Tao Te Ching. The word 'Zen' slipped into common parlance to mean relaxed or laid back and was even used in advertising copy. There is a perfume with that name to this day. At airports everywhere, you could find the latest offerings of superstars of the spiritual circuit such as Deepak Chopra who had accumulated sufficient wealth from all his 'spiritual' activity to own a private jet! The striking contrast between the behaviour of this 'successful' spiritual businessman with the absence of greed and ostentation of the generation that preceded him – most members of which made no claims to being spiritual – tells you that by then the tables had been turned upside down and the word 'spirituality' had started to lose all meaning.

From the very start, I had deep misgivings about this ferment of activity but couldn't justify them to myself. Surely the democratization of spirituality was a good thing, I thought. My instincts, however, kept flashing red until I realized that this tidal wave of spiritual offerings was missing a fundamental ingredient – the sense of the sacred. This element, I realized, is such a fundamental aspect of spirituality that in its absence you have a situation where there is 'water, water everywhere and not a drop to drink'. The movement that carried millions in its wake had vulgarized spirituality beyond any claim to be what it is. Spirituality is rooted in the personal experience of the sacred or we are talking about something else altogether. As a student in Montreal in the mid 1960's I could still remember going to second-hand bookshops where two dusty shelves would be allotted to second-hand esoteric literature and, if I found what I was looking for, it was like stumbling on the holy grail. I would return home with these books as though I had a treasure in my hands. To this day that collection is still my most precious possession.

What I am suggesting is that in the oddness of that behaviour, the sense of the sacred was present. The child-like awe and wonder that I was fortunate enough to experience as I turned the pages of those books, was the chink in my habitually egoic and unconscious carapace that permitted some light to enter my being. There are no words to describe the elation of those moments. Monastic chants and holy music in cathedrals are designed to evoke those same emotions. There is no spiritual life without this. The special wonder and 'openness' I refer to is what Zen master Shunryu Suzuki called 'beginners mind'. It is also the reason why Jesus appealed to us to become 'as little children' (Matthew 18:3). If the sense of the sacred is absent, a spiritual experience risks becoming a mere figment of the imagination or a fabrication of the emotions that the ego will instantly elevate to something it is not. This is not an attempt on my part to devalue or impugn all that falls under the umbrella of the New Age. There are some rogues and charlatans, there is no doubt, but there are also some very sincere and well-intentioned people who do good things. They must be applauded. I am just suggesting that unless the sense of the sacred is present no amount of goodwill can make an activity spiritual. 'Darshan' in the Hindu tradition, is the transmission of a blessing that only a person of genuine spiritual stature can give. Such people are rare.

There is another consideration. By going mainstream, spirituality also created an unfortunate form of clannishness, a divide between those who saw themselves as 'initiates' of sorts and those who were not. In reality, this distinction was entirely illusory, but clannishness persisted, giving rise to certain attitudes among some 'initiates' that were the very opposite of spiritual. The absence of humility should have been a red light. The egoic temptation to think more highly of oneself and project an image that separates one from the herd is often hard to resist. Few do. The truth is that there are good and worthy people who have no interest in spirituality and less worthy people who think, write and talk about it all the time. A striking example would be the case of Marianne Williamson, a third time Democratic candidate to be president of the U.S, who, despite building a long career preaching love, compassion and forgiveness and writing best-selling books on the subject, has been revealed by her campaign staff to be a 'tyrant' given to outbursts of 'uncontrollable rage'. The State director of the Ohio campaign described her behaviour as "belittling, abusive, dehumanizing and unacceptable". Faux gurus such as this do an enormous disservice to the already ill-understood concept of spirituality, re-enforcing the widespread scepticism that surrounds the subject.

But to get back to a historical perspective. The 1960's was the era of Carnaby Street fashions, Swinging London and the iconic rock festival of Woodstock, USA. Those who wanted to be in tune with their time were encouraged to make a pilgrimage to San Francisco, the mecca of the 'peace and love' movement. During this whole period there was an unspoken understanding that this liberated generation and the hippie movement in general, represented 'seekers' of a new, less materialistic and more spiritual way to live. Hippie communities sprung up everywhere. Although much of it was heartfelt and genuine, the whimsical and disorganized nature of the movement was not realistic and failed to give it coherence. It inevitably fell apart.

By the late 1970's 'spirituality' had really come into its own. EST (Erhard Seminar Training) had become a hugely successful combination of motivational training laced with a hodgepodge of spiritual principles borrowed from multiple spiritual traditions. Middle-class professionals from all walks of life were prepared to have themselves locked up over a long weekend in a hotel ballroom and be harassed by trainers so as to arrive at a state of 'self-actualization' (a fast-track form of enlightenment referred to as 'getting it'). Men left their wives, women left their husbands, men and women left their jobs, all in the name of becoming 'more authentically themselves'. Whether this was the case or not is open to question, but millions of people believed it was. Werner Erhard, the founder, became a celebrity of the Human Potential Movement and the era of industrial scale commodification of spirituality was launched. The collective brand of this new era was the 'New Age'.

In the meantime, it is worth remembering what we are discussing here. At stake was whether this 'spiritual renaissance' could bring about change in the world. Was this the promise of 'the Age of Aquarius' finally coming into being? Were we going to sing, love and dance our way to a happier, freer and more joyous world, as the hippies believed? After a long history of violence, cruelty and ignorance was mankind on the brink of a breakthrough to some form of higher consciousness. Unfortunately not. Our age-old demons were still with us. Instead of seeing a weakening of human egoism during this ferment of spiritual activity, as might have been expected, the 1980's and beyond heralded an era of material greed, conservatism and secularity unlike any other in recent history. The dark suits and short haircuts were back with a vengeance signaling the advent of a period where 'masters of the universe' would take over the helm of business and finance for the next forty years, some of the consequences of which I outlined in earlier chapters.

Why, after a moment of much promise, did this happen? I can only answer that question by suggesting that the unique and hope-filled period of the 1960s' and 70's was not a deep-seated spiritual revolution as we had supposed at the time, but just an exuberant reaction and much-needed liberation from the grim and restrictive post-war years. An interest in spirituality had indeed come to the fore during that time (albeit, in the disjointed ways I discussed earlier) but taken as a whole, the movement lacked sufficient depth to effect lasting change. Much of it was theatre. People went through the motions, they 'talked the talk' (some very convincingly), but the demons of our egoic condition that had never really disappeared prevent us from being able to genuinely 'walk the walk'. In fact, a short time later, those same demons were back in the driver's seat as never before. The world was not more spiritual at the end of the 20th century than it had been fifty years before, arguably less so when you subtract all the 'noise' (although I know many people will disagree with me on this).

Why do I say this? Because during this period and unlike any time in the past, spirituality had found a niche in the world, it has been 'normalized' and gone mainstream. No longer the realm of 'outsiders', it had been accommodated by the status quo and become an activity like any other – a job, career or way of life for some, a profitable form of 'business' for others. In a word, it had become fully integrated into the modern world.

What harm is there in that, you can ask? None, except that spirituality is NOT a human activity like any other. That's the whole point. It stands outside of the status quo for a very good reason; it is there to change it. Spirituality, wholly incompatible with the level of consciousness of the egoic status quo, is anything but normative. It has the potential to change the direction of human life but cannot under any circumstances become integrated into it.

Before we go any further, let us examine for a moment this nebulous concept we call spirituality.

At a strictly esoteric level, spirituality is the experience of TRANSCENDENCE, a moment where consciousness breaks out of its normal parameters to afford glimpses of a reality unlike that to which a person is accustomed. These are sometimes referred to as moments of 'higher consciousness' or 'peak experience' and they are typically fleeting. No matter how sudden or short it is, if it is genuine, it will change a person's perspective on life forever. There are many notable examples throughout history, usually among writers, artists, thinkers, philosophers and poets. In the narrowest and strictest terms, without transcendence there is no spirituality. Colin Wilson's most notable work, *The Outsider*, was a compendium of individuals in modern times, from Vincent Van Gogh to Dostoevsky, who had experienced moments of higher consciousness describing how their deeper insights into the nature of reality pushed them to the margins of society. That would still be the case today.

However, I would like to suggest another perspective that may seem to contradict much of what I have said earlier. My reasoning is as follows.

The modern world is in a state of emergency. 'The centre cannot hold' and 'things ARE falling apart', to paraphrase W.B.Yeats. For this reason, there is an urgent need to widen the definition of spirituality to encompass a less esoteric and more workable way for it to be applied in the world. This is the condition, referred to in the opening paragraphs of this chapter, where I gave examples of the human spirit infiltrating people's lives in small, non-mystical but vitally important ways. It's at this level, I am suggesting, that there is a realistic possibility that change can occur on the scale that is necessary because, as we know full well, billions of people in the world are not going to become 'aware' in the classic sense and we are fast running out of time. The positive news is that there are encouraging signs that this more applicable form of spiritual activity is developing on a larger scale than appearances would suggest. Eckhart Tolle, for example, whose spiritual teaching is both deep and practicable, has sold tens of millions of books in 50 languages and fills auditoriums all over the world. More on this in the next chapter.

But going back for a moment to what happened in the 1960's and 70's, I will leave it to the reader to decide whether or not 'spirituality', by any definition, lends itself to commercial treatment of the kind I described earlier or treatment of any sort other than that which brings a person closer to the sacred and nobody knows how to engineer that at will. When a 'peak experience' takes place, it tends to happen by surprise and people refer to it as an act of 'grace' – attaching a label to a phenomenon that is essentially mysterious. Meanwhile, a few words from the pages of a scripture, a Bach fugue in a church or a beautiful sunset can be as powerful a catalyst to spiritual awakening as sitting at the foot of a 'guru' or diligently participating in workshops where the principles of spirituality are often being taught by those who understand the theory but rarely embody the practice, Furthermore, it can happen to anybody, saint or sinner alike. There is no hierarchy of merit in the spiritual world.

Meanwhile, it is important to understand that in spite of the fact that the word 'teaching' is so often used with regard to spirituality, in reality it CANNOT be taught; it can only be communicated by means of the living example of what words refer to. "Truth is lived not taught", stated Hermann Hesse. Theoretical knowledge alone lacks transformational power because the essential vector of spirituality is the soul not the mind. Anyone who has been in the presence of a genuinely wise being knows the difference. In the case of Jesus, all who crossed his path were transfixed by the manifestation of other worldliness in human form. Such was the power of his presence ('being') that two thousand years later, his message, recorded by his followers and available to us in the form of testaments, can still lift our consciousness. Jesus was a unique example, you could say, but there is a long lineage of sages and saints from different spiritual traditions, some of whom preceded him but others that came afterwards, that offered a very similar message to his. However, one must be mindful of the fact that when we look for the LIVING example of a spiritual teaching today, veritable sages are rare.

This should not be a source of discouragement, however. Nothing can change the fact that we are 'made in the image of God' meaning that the seeds of 'being' exists within us all. If those seeds are nurtured, if a person is not distracted by false promises, if he or she can be, 'as little children' – open, humble and sincere - then there's a great likelihood that providence will come to their assistance and show them the way forward. There are many obstacles on the path because the world is a challenging context in which to seek wisdom. But more and more people have understood this and are rising to the challenge. In the view of Eckhart Tolle, the situation in the world has never been more polarized. On the one hand, we are confronted with examples of 'collective psychosis' (to use C.G Jung's term) on a massive scale. On the other, there is more 'awareness' in the world today than ever before.

So, it can be said that in fits and starts we ARE evolving. The immense potential of the human spirit, overlooked for millennia, is beginning to stir. But unlike the 1960's and 70's, it is not by colourful displays of spiritual exuberance that this is happening – which is why we hear so little about it and underestimate its scale – but by people willing to dedicate their lives to humble and steadfast service to others and the planet. You have only to witness the large number of people who live self-sacrificing lives working for NGO's and other humanitarian organizations in some of the harshest environments in the world to know this. The large number of educators and health workers are doing the same closer to home. Encouraging also is the fact that we are seeing more and more highly qualified members of the younger generation turning their backs on the opportunity for rapid self-enrichment to get involved in 'alternative' ventures of a more meaningful nature (agro-ecology, for example). These practical and pragmatic activities are precisely what is required today and has an undoubted spiritual component to them. This is no time for 'other-worldliness', the focus must now be on 'this-worldliness'.

I have far greater confidence in the depth, scale and staying power of the movement that is afoot today than in the one that preceded it sixty years ago – though an argument can be made that the earlier one was a necessary preliminary stage. I can't say for sure.

6

HOPE

While most people still believe that hope for the future resides in the resolution of the socio-economic and political challenges, we face in the world today and there are many (outlined in earlier chapters), I disagree. What we witness today are the consequences of causes that lie in the distant past and have little to do with recent events, bad as they are. The essential underlying reasons for things being what they are, is, and has always been our egoic condition that reduces the meaning and purpose of life to individual and collective self-interest. This condition is a cancer of the soul and we are dying from it.

In modern times, the veritable elephant in the room, that, again, is a symptom of our collective egoism and not a cause, is all that falls under the umbrella of 'business-as-usual', the cynical label we attach to a highly cynical reality. Despite overwhelming evidence of the harm inflicted on society and the planet by these destructive practices, they continue to flourish unconstrained. Why? Because to one degree or another we are all complicit in creating them and are unable (or unwilling) to disentangle ourselves from this self-destructive nexus. At this late hour we shouldn't need Greta Thunberg to urge us to heed Gandhi's famed call "to be the change you wish to see in the world."

The question we should all be asking ourselves is, how can I avoid being part of this outdated and destructive paradigm? Is a different vision of life possible?

The answer is an unequivocal YES - and I say this because a growing number of people are moving in a new direction. Narrowing the purpose of life to its most elemental and utilitarian aspects (economic growth at all costs, self-aggrandizement, a disregard for moral and spiritual values and so on) belongs in the past. It is "yesterday's logic", as Peter Drucker once observed; a short-sighted vision that comes with destructive consequences to our humanity and our habitat. In addition, in the rush to satisfy pragmatic and self-serving ambitions, we continue to overlook the ever-present potential to transcend our egoic condition and fulfil our potential as human beings, a far more important aspiration.

It should be clear, therefore, that the re-organization of the pieces on the same socio-political and economic chessboard is NOT the answer. Many still pin their hopes on the promise of technology. They, too, will be disappointed. Finding a scientific solution to a moral and spiritual problem is clearly delusional. 'Man does not live by technology alone' although many people believe that we do. In truth, we require inputs of a very different nature. If sustainable ways of living on earth are to emerge, they must do so from an entirely NEW CONCEPTION of our role and place in the universe and such an adjustment can only come from acquiring a spiritual vision of life.

The problem, however, is that most people don't have a proper understanding of what spirituality is. Its unfortunate association with conventional religion has been the source of much confusion causing people in large numbers to throw out the baby of spirituality with the bathwater of religion. It is important to understand that scientific rationalism rooted in logic, the prevailing mindset, and the reason many dismiss the whole question of spirituality, addresses quite DIFFERENT needs. You cannot expect science or reason to embrace issues that are neither scientific nor rational. "The human heart and body do not obey the rationality that our modern world worships. Science does not bring morality, does not bring love, does not bring justice," – we are reminded by Jacob Needleman, Professor of Philosophy at San Francisco University. All of this belongs to the domain of the scientifically immeasurable and spiritual.

What those who have given up on religion need to understand is that conventional religion and spirituality have little in common. Great spiritual figures such as Jesus Christ and Siddartha Gautama (the Buddha) who inspired two of the world's great 'religions', did not have a hand in creating the monolithic entities that carry their names. Can one imagine for a single instant that Jesus would have sponsored the power, pomp and opulence of the Papacy? Or that the Buddha would have wanted there to be a monastic hierarchy of monks in saffron robes who blow horns, spin prayer wheels and prostrate themselves in his name? Long-standing and admired as these institutions are today, none of this was the creation of Jesus or the Buddha but of those who came hundreds of years after their time.

The single purpose of the messages of those two great spiritual teachers was to AWAKEN people to their spiritual nature, which is to say, to who and what they are in essence. In the simplest terms, their teachings can be considered instruction manuals on how to live our lives, so as to be able to experience the full potential of being human. After all, we spent years at school accepting instructions with regard to almost everything else in life. Why not the most important one of all? The teachings were also directed towards making us understand that this higher manifestation of ourselves was possible HERE ON EARTH – not in 'heaven' or in the confines of a monastery. They were intended to have a PRACTICAL application in our everyday lives; spiritual awakening being a personal experience in the here and now, not some reward in the next life for our virtue in this one.

Spirituality is not a belief system. It is not dependent on 'faith', prayers or liturgy. It's a deeper understanding of how we actually function. Neuroscientist Sam Harris, emphasizing the practical and empirical nature of a spiritual awakening, had this to say: "The promise of spiritual life – indeed the very thing that makes it spiritual – is that there are truths about the mind that we are better off knowing. What we need to become happier and make the world a better place is not more pious illusions but a clear understanding of the way things are." Quite true, but unfortunately by replacing INNER experience with OUTER rituals, the institutionalization of 'pious illusions' by conventional religion has deformed the whole notion of spirituality. It would not be an exaggeration to say that nothing in our psycho/spiritual evolution has had such a far-reaching effect on our civilization. No single factor in history has nourished our ignorance and installed a deep-seated state of unconsciousness with regard to spiritual issues – creating brutal divisiveness within societies as well as conflict between societies – than conventional religion.

Another misperception, wrongly promoted by conventional Christianity, is that we are inherently too sinful and 'fallen' to be redeemable in this life. This bleak and censorious notion is not only incorrect but serves to alienate and discourage people in the hundreds of millions from having anything to do with religion or spirituality. In truth, the whole concept of sinfulness or being 'fallen' arises from an entirely erroneous interpretation of the scriptures. The true meaning of the words 'man is made in the image of God', is that humanity is both a reflection and an expression of the source of all creation (i.e. 'God') itself. This extraordinarily important fact has never been properly understood. We only seem to be able to grasp this notion in dualistic terms – a 'God' who orders (or fails to order) our existence on the one hand, and mankind who submits to its fate on the other. This misconception has hobbled humanity for millennia virtually guaranteeing that no change in our spiritual condition could take place – worse still, it has had the effect of pushing us further into faithlessness and despair – hence the deadening secularity of life as we know it today.

So, how can we break out of this seemingly fated impasse? In a word, 'self-awareness'.

While the state of (spiritual) 'awareness' is a psychological condition of paramount importance, it is nowhere to be found in textbooks on psychology. Conventional psychology and science in general fail to acknowledge that there exists a dimension of consciousness other than our normal waking consciousness, that is deeply transformational. This condition, one that can loosely be described as 'being conscious of being conscious', has been recognized by all the great spiritual traditions as the fundamental object of spiritual practice – and its absence, the greatest obstacle to awakening. Sam Harris sums it up by stating: "If you are thinking without knowing that you are thinking, you are confused about who and what you are."

It is for this reason that our normal (waking) condition is often referred to as 'sleep'. In the Hindu tradition, for example, they call spiritual awakening 'self-realization', suggesting that to realize the self (to become who you are) is the single and most important objective in life. We are incomplete without it. Most people would claim that this is all nonsense because they know perfectly well 'who they are'. Unfortunately, the history of mankind tells you otherwise. All the spiritual traditions that exist came into being for one reason and one reason only, to guide humanity towards this particular form of self-knowledge. It is the pre-eminent function of being human. Without this understanding, human existence becomes chaotic and self-destructive as our past and present history so clearly demonstrates. Living out our time on earth not knowing who we are and what the potential of being truly human can represent, should be an appalling prospect to most people – and yet, few give it a passing thought. As a result, this gaping hole in our understanding of ourselves is a dysfunction that gnaws away at the foundations of our civilization.

In what way would self-awareness change that? The moment we see that in our habitual state of consciousness we have little control of our thoughts and feelings and tend to identify with everything and anything that comes up on the screen of our consciousness, the 'noise' ceases momentarily and something else arises in its place. That 'something else' embodies the seeds of self-awareness. If we allow these seeds to develop, the shifting sands of our identity eventually settles into a deeper and more permanent sense of who we are. This is experienced as extraordinarily liberating. Furthermore, this deeper and more stable sense of self is typically accompanied by powerful insights, the one most often cited by people being the sensation that everything in the universe is RELATED and that all things are ONE.

There is absolutely nothing new here, however. Nothing of what I have said here is my own.

All this has been written and re-written in different ways for thousands of years. This knowledge is embedded in all the scriptures including Christianity, but mostly un-acknowledged because their esoteric significance is rarely understood. The perception of the essential UNITY of the universe in a non-metaphysical sense (laws of relativity etc.) was embraced by physics a long time ago. But from the psychological point of view, the essential importance of a moment of 'awakening' (and a moment is usually all you will get) is the discovery that there exists a deeper dimension to life than the familiar parameters of the rational mind – and when that happens, a person will never see things in quite the same way again.

Can any of this be explained in rational terms? The answer is, NO. Reason denies us access to this level of perception. It is an intellectual construct going back hundreds of years that has imprinted on our civilization the belief in a strictly empirical interpretation of reality. The influence of René Descartes, who lived 400 years ago, as I mentioned earlier, was a critical turning point in this respect. But the Cartesian view of reality is narrow, short-sighted and inadequate. Reason (unlike, say, 'Love'), is not a universal absolute. It's just one faculty of the intellect among others. Don't expect reason to give you an insight into the ultimate reality of things (although the fact that many people believe that it does is a major part of the problem). Rationality has vitally important uses. We owe the physical infrastructure of the modern world to reason. There is no denying the spectacular advances of science but let us – 'render unto Caesar that which is Caesar's' (science and technology) and 'to God the things that are God's' (the spiritual principles of life) Matthew 21:22, and cease to confuse the two. The fact remains that a purely rational view of life is exceedingly limiting because it fails to account for the most important things in life, those that can't be touched or measured. We can survive without much of the material infrastructure that exists today (as millions still do in many parts of the world) but who would want to live, so much as a single day, in a world devoid of love and compassion?

If we can accept for a moment the irrational principle that the 'self' we experience in moments of awareness is our true human identity then it necessarily corresponds to that dimension that is 'made in the image of God' – which is another way of saying that our fundamental human constitution is made of the SAME ELEMENTS as the universal source of all life that we call 'God' (as touched on earlier). It also tells us that knowing who and what we are, is not determined by the mind or the brain, as we are inclined to believe, but by 'consciousness' alone (which is neither one nor the other). The 'consciousness', that science is still struggling to understand or define, is a distinct phenomenon and the one that mystics of all traditions over the entire span of human history agree in saying is the critical factor in the struggle to 'awake'. What does this signify? From a psychological point of view, the awakened 'self' gets to experience that it does NOT exist in a random cosmos but is an intrinsic and related part of a meaningful WHOLE. This 'coming home' so to speak, of the 'self' is a psychological re-birth of extraordinary importance. It turns on its head every preconceived notion we might have had about the meaning and purpose of life.

This is how Jacob Needleman described such a moment: "For one fleeting second, an indescribable, subtle force touched every cell in my body, every hope in my heart, every question in my mind. Or should I say simply, something truly sacred appeared in me and disappeared even as it appeared. Like a thousand fine particles of silent light."

When Jesus said: "Deny thyself, take up your cross and follow me" (Matthew 16:24) he was urging people to abandon the egoic 'self' so as to experience a moment of meaningful union that Jacob Needleman described above. Jesus insisted on this in the Gospels because moving away from the illusory egoic 'self' amounts to the lifting of the blinders that prevent us from experiencing the extraordinary beauty and perfection – yes, perfection, of life as it really is beyond the superficial, highly imperfect and reductionist version that we have been educated and conditioned to believe in. The significance of this is incalculable. Our actions become harmful to ourselves, others and the planet when we are unanchored to our real selves and cut off from that reality. All the ugliness and cruelty of life arises from that condition. The state of the world today suggests that we are at a critical inflection point. We move beyond the egoic 'self' towards greater 'awareness' or our civilization will fall apart – and we don't have much time.

This can be written in stone. I defy anyone to propose a model of the future that doesn't incorporate these elements. We have tried all the expedients that the egoic vision of life has to offer and none of them work.

Like the transformation of base metals into gold, 'awakening' has an alchemical effect on our beings such that everything becomes redolent with meaning – not from what we DO, which is where the un-awakened world looks for meaning, but from who we ARE. At those moments, the playing field becomes level and a president is no more privileged than a janitor. It is reported that even some prisoners serving life sentences on death row have been able to experience moments of intense happiness, as did certain individuals in the Nazi concentration camps. No more precious resource exists than what we carry in our souls, and it is readily available to every one of us, should we only know it. More crucial than inventing the internet or going to Mars, getting to know who we are (as defined earlier) is the single most important objective in life for an individual and the only collective destiny for mankind. Colonizing space will do nothing to heal our psychological wounds. It will do nothing to bring us closer to the reality of who we are. The outer world can only be changed by our inner world.

Dialing back the narrative a little, I would like to take a closer look for a moment into the nature of the (un-awakened) egoic consciousness.

In our habitual psychological condition, is experienced through the prism of the ego. As this is how we have been conditioned to relate to the world from infancy, it goes largely unquestioned and considered endemic to the human condition. For this reason, we accept as normal that our psychological condition is essentially haphazard, unstable and incapable of transcendence. Normal to us also are the symptoms that come with this condition. Discouragement can rapidly follow on the tails of elation, pain on that of pleasure, nothing we do can seem to provide us with an enduring sense of fulfillment and for some, the lingering sensation that life is devoid of meaning never entirely disappears. Acknowledged or not, the vast majority of people on earth experience varying degrees of the psychological 'malaise' that the Buddha called 'dukkha'.

Eric Fromm, the eminent German psychologist, stated that it is not just individuals but society as a whole that has become dysfunctional to the point of collective insanity - a condition that is not perceived as such because it has become normative, he concluded. Noted spiritual teacher Jiddu Krishnamurti would seem to confirm this view when he stated: "It is no measure of health to be adjusted to a sick society." The fact that our dysfunctions are normalized means that we are unable to identify them. The consequences, however, are serious. At one end of the spectrum you have the 'normative' pathological patterns that we are accustomed to (at the origin of a whole series of anomalies we take for granted) and at the other, the extreme pathology of psychopaths like Joseph Stalin, Adolf Hitler and Vladimir Putin who are capable of unleashing unspeakable suffering on the world. Every nuance of human dysfunction exists in between these extremes.

Is this our fate? Is there nothing we can do? The answer is that while we consider our egoic identity to be who we are, all this is unavoidable.

Simply put, what we identify as the ego is an IMPOSTER. It has no real psychological foundation. It's a reality that owes its existence to nothing more substantial than the ABSENCE of an awareness that a deeper 'self' exists. But for as long as this illusion persists, the world cannot be other than what it is. We go round and round in circles, repeating the same mistakes, are subject to the same delusions while experiencing the same succession of 'triumphs and disappointments. It's a treadmill of meaninglessness.

Furthermore, by experiencing itself as an entity unconnected to anything greater than itself, the egoic condition is necessarily insecure and defensive. Selfishness, greed, pride, jealousy and vanity are just defensive reactions to this essential vulnerability. They are DISTORTIONS of our true nature, nothing more. But as long as the ego drives our existence, these demons will always be with us. This, too, is unavoidable.

Does this mean that the human condition is a 'cosmic joke', as many believe? Absolutely not.

The opening lines of *A Course In Miracles* by Helen Schucman reads: "Nothing real can be threatened, nothing unreal exists", perfectly summarizes the underlying reality of our lives. A person who is (spiritually) whole cannot be hurt by the delusions of the world. The line that follows: "Therein lies the peace of God", indicates that all human fulfilment and happiness arises from the experience of this truth.

Therefore, another way to live IS open to us. St Augustine of Hippo in his sermon on 'Love' on Easter Saturday in the year AD 407 famously declared: "Love and do what you will", a statement that must have astonished his followers at the time and would still do so today. But what St Augustine meant by those words is perhaps the key to an understanding of how the deeper 'self' functions – the word 'love', as it was used in the ancient scriptural writings being the approximate equivalent of 'awareness' (higher consciousness) in spiritual terminology today. Understood in this way, St Augustine was declaring that in a state of 'awareness' a person is free to act as he or she wishes because, devoid of the ego, the motivations of a such a person can only be positive. This should be a welcome piece of good news. Moral restraint, it is implied by St Augustine's words, is only necessary when we act from the egoic self.

Civilization has its moral codes for one reason only, to curb the harmful excesses of egoism by establishing standards of good conduct that are universally recognized and respected. It is a vital pact we impose on ourselves to make life livable in the inherent chaos arising from unconstrained egoic unconsciousness. It should be noted that the roots of the 'moral' code that we impose on ourselves is nothing more than the natural elements of our spiritual essence. The only thing that is unnatural is the necessity to do so. This pact of moral conduct takes the form of local and international systems of law and order that are enforced within a society by police forces and between societies by military means.

But as moral restraint is not a natural impulse to the egoic self, the whole structure remains essentially fragile. It can break down at any moment, as we have seen with tragic consequences in the past and are seeing again today with Putin's war in Ukraine. Human evil then has no limits. What St Augustine was telling us is that spiritual wholeness alters our consciousness in such a way that this would no longer be possible. He understood that 'love' (awareness) being the highest manifestation of what it is to be human meant that right action could not be anything other than natural and spontaneous implying that there is no fundamentally 'bad' or 'evil' dimension to our essential nature. We are not made, in equal parts, in the image of God and the Devil!

That is why, moments before he died on the cross, referring to those who had crucified him, Jesus said: "Forgive them, they know not what they do." (Luke 23:24) – words of an enormous significance. People who know not who they are, 'know not what they do' and therefore do things for which, in an absolute sense, they cannot be held responsible. If a person knows no better, he or she can do no better. We live in a universe where the overwhelming majority of people are NOT connected to an inner self and go about their lives not 'knowing who they are' and, by extension, 'what they do'; not necessarily in harmful ways, of course – most people are well meaning – but lacking awareness we harm without the intention to harm, hence John Stuart Mill's warning of the danger of people living passive and unconscious lives – earlier in the book.

G I Gurdjieff, one of the most influential spiritual teachers of the 20th century, put this in very clear terms when he stated: "People are machines, What can you expect from machines? The unconscious actions of millions of machines must necessarily result in destruction. IT IS PRECISELY IN UNCONSCIOUS INVOLUNTARY MANIFESTATIONS THAT ALL EVIL LIES".

It could be argued with some validity that the social, political and ecological reality of the world as we know it, is nothing more than an accumulation of unintended consequences arising from our 'unconscious involuntary manifestations'. No one group of people intentionally set out to establish economic injustice in the world or destroy the ecological balance of the planet. But if future generations are to endure in a post carbon/post-capitalist world (or some combination of the two) they must imperatively 'know what they do'. The survival of mankind in any recognizable form will depend on this.

The good news is that this is not how things have to be. We are not fated to continue down this perilous path. We have a choice, and that choice is to develop a spiritual vision of life.

But what if we fail?

On the 6th of January 2021, encouraged by the then president Donald Trump, the Capitol in Washington was stormed by his armed followers. Six lives were lost, many police officers were injured, some members of Congress narrowly avoided being killed and the symbol of American democracy was defiled as never before. This is a perfect example of 'unconscious, involuntary manifestations' leading to evil by people 'who know not what they do'. It would have surely led to far greater evil if the insurrection had succeeded. Fortunately, it didn't. But if a person is inclined to believe that spirituality is an abstraction with little relevance to events such as this, it would be time to reconsider. It is PRECISELY at such pivotal moments in history that the question of spirituality takes on all its meaning. When faced with outbursts of collective madness, it is humankind's foremost line of defence. Let us not forget that in Germany in 1930's a deranged megalomaniac similar in breed to Putin, took the reins of one of the most civilized societies on earth with the promise to purify the human race and make 'Germany Great Again'. We know of the horrors that followed.

But there are no lack of precedents. Paranoia on a pathological scale caused Stalin in Russia to murder 20 million of his own people, as did Pol Pot when he systematically executed a quarter of the population of Cambodia. The Two World Wars cost the world well in excess of 100 million lives. Deranged authoritarians have brought rack and ruin to nations such as Iraq, Libya, Venezuela and Zimbabwe while cruel authoritarian regimes prevail in Iran and Myanmar. The destructive capacity of unconscious individuals has no limits and can cause human suffering on an unimaginable scale. Facing defeat on the battlefield, Putin's war is now directed at inflicting a maximum of despair and suffering on the civilian population of Ukraine, a war crime and a human abomination. My generation, born right after the Second World War, thought we would never see horror on this scale again. We naively believed that humanity had evolved beyond such things. We were wrong. Putin's conduct of this war is the re-appearance of evil in Europe in its most primal form and the world is experiencing a bitter and unexpected a wake-up call. We can no longer think that this won't happen again. It will, and with greater frequency if conditions on earth, due to geo-political tensions, societal breakdown or climate change, become untenable – a perfectly plausible scenario. We are seeing signs of societal tensions and febrility everywhere.

There is no one who better understood the danger of humanity, left to its own devices in conditions of moral deprivation than 17th century philosopher, Thomas Hobbes. Instead of an inner spiritual authority placing limits on man's cruelty to man, he saw this as the duty of a central authority in society. In its absence, he described man's lot as a: "War of every man against every man – no place for industry because the fruit thereof is uncertain, and consequently no culture of the earth. No arts, No letters. And which is worse of all, continual fear and danger of violent death."

Present day examples of the latent anarchy that Hobbes referred to are not as rare as we might think. The increasingly secular environment in which we find ourselves has caused a marked degeneration in standards of moral conduct. The veneer of civilization that we depend upon on is in constant jeopardy. Before January 6th 2021, who would have believed it possible that armed insurrectionists would storm the Capitol of the United States of America? In post-pandemic

America, who would believe that marauding bands of thieves would invade stores and loot them in broad daylight and are gone before law enforcement can arrive (ORC, organized retail crime, they call it) prompting retailers to shut down stores all over the country. This is only a short step away from Mad Max. Who can properly comprehend the fact that seemingly ordinary individuals, mostly young, choose to slaughter innocent people, very often children in schools, with tragic regularity in America? (606 mass shootings in 2022 until the time of writing in November, 2022.) The protective veneer of civility and good conduct has become wafer thin and it's not a ramping up of law enforcement that can make any difference. In the face of an INTERNAL breakdown of our moral and spiritual constitution, external agents of change are ineffective.

Hobbes, it must be said, had a particularly grim view of the human condition and was almost certainly an atheist. Since his time, social scientists have argued endlessly over his conclusions without coming to a definite verdict on the matter. As there is much evidence to support his beliefs, this is understandable. However, standing in stark opposition to such ideas is the Perennial Philosophy based on a body of knowledge stretching back thousands of years expressing an opposing view to that of Hobbes. On what evidence? Disparate traditions from different cultures and epochs have come to remarkably similar conclusions with regard to the existence of a spiritual reality. This is circumstantial evidence of a very compelling sort.

The point is that the Hobbesian view of life is a HOPE-LESS one that offers no possibility of fundamental change in human behaviour. Enforcement of right conduct by coercive means is not the same thing. Coercive systems, as we have seen over and over again in history, can break down very easily. It is time to move beyond this and settle the critical question - are we made in the image of God or not? Are we spiritual beings as a long lineage of our greatest thinkers believe or are we random egos scrambling for survival in a hostile universe? If it's the former, no need for coercion, if it's the latter, we depend on it entirely. Paying lip service to Christianity or going through the motions of spiritual practice in the rituals of conventional religion, changes little in this respect. To rectify the situation, it has become absolutely vital that the Perennial Philosophy should cease to be viewed as the exclusive province of monks, mystics or the spiritually inclined. The teaching it represents should be re-defined as a fundamental element of a STANDARD EDUCATION in the same way as history or algebra – and, most importantly, that the values and vision it embodies be viewed, not just as noble ideals, but as a practical and PRAGMATIC way to conduct our lives.

For purposes of simplification, we should look at this as the opposing forces of spirituality and secularity facing off in a high stakes existential tug-of-war where it is imperative that humanity's better angels prevail. Life on the planet, as we know it, hangs in the balance. I would be dishonest on my part if I didn't say that, as things are, there isn't much cause for optimism. Owing to the rapid evolution of technology in the last 50 years, secularity has all but taken over the world. However, the extraordinary reactive power of the human spirit in extreme moments must never be underestimated. There is reason for hope.

I know that concepts such as 'higher consciousness', 'awareness' and spirituality in general that I continuously refer to in this book are unfamiliar to most people. Except in rare instances, spiritual principles were not what they were taught at home, school or university – at least, not in the way I have expressed it here. It is unlikely that this would be a common topic of conversation among family, friends and acquaintances either. Should it then all be dismissed as fanciful nonsense with little connection to reality? It is understandable that people would think that. After all, nothing in their everyday life would seem to bear any of this out - but it would be a colossal error to do so.

The reason is simple.

It is precisely our 'unconsciousness' (as defined earlier), our 'not knowing what we do' that exposes the shaky and dysfunctional egoic edifice on which our lives are founded, for what it is. It is vital to see this because while the ego holds us in its thrall we are stuck, nothing can change. All the wisdom teachings concur on this point. Awareness is the only means of seeing through this stubborn and perilous illusion. The good news is that a small but growing number of people have understood this. There is a movement afoot that has nothing in common with the colourful dalliance with spirituality of the 1960's. Quite the contrary. Far from being a passing fad of the younger generations, these are people of all ages from all walks of life and in ever greater quantities who have seen the writing on the wall.

Nonetheless, it would be understandable for a person who has no familiarity with any of this to ask – in what ways would awareness change their life?

The answer is ....IN EVERY WAY.

There is not a single choice they would make in life that would not be modified, in small or big ways by greater awareness – the kind of work they do, the environment they would choose to live in, the wife, husband or partner they would wish to share their life with and the kind of friendships they would seek. Their habits, attitudes and interests would be correspondingly quite different also. With respect to the habitual demons of greed, pride, egoism, jealousy, vanity etc., the greater the awareness, the less of a hold they would have on them. Why be greedy, selfish or jealous when their real self leaves them feeling whole and wanting of nothing? What need for pride when there is nothing ultimately for them to prove to anyone? What could be vainer than vanity itself under the circumstances?

It's not that we suddenly break with deeply ingrained habits of egoism. That would not be possible. What happens in the first instance is that a modified notion of what serves our best interest takes its place. This gradual shift in our understanding of the meaning and purpose of life has the effect of altering our behaviour in small but significant ways at first. For example, we come to the understanding that we need far less of what the material world has to offer to experience a greater degree of satisfaction in our lives. Similarly, at the macro level, we open our eyes to the fact that individual and collective egoism are taking us to the ecological limits of what this planet can bear. Who can fail to see that? The slightest shift in our perception of these issues will bring about a significant modification in our behaviour. This has now become critical. In a previous book, in order to make what I was saying more palatable and avoid the word 'spiritual', I referred to this as 'positive selfishness'. But it isn't really of any importance what individual words or labels we use; it is the truth of the message that matters.

Unfortunately, we are not where we need to be on all this.

The predominantly egoic condition of humanity still involves the vast majority of us in a quixotic struggle to assert our interests as though life is a zero-sum game. It never works, of course, because there are no prizes to be won in the race of life. This becomes ever clearer as we near the end of it and see that whatever we might have accomplished will soon be as 'dust to dust' in terms of the illusory pride we may derive from those accomplishments. Steve Jobs is rumoured to have said before his premature departure: "I realize that all the recognition and wealth that I took so much pride in have paled and become meaningless in the face of my death."

The Buddha was a keen psychologist and well understood our egoic condition as long ago as 600 BC. In his 'Four Noble Truths' he emphasized the futility of all egoic expectations, telling us that, dissatisfaction ('dukkha', in Sanskrit) stalks the egoic self like a shadow. There is no escaping it. Desire follows on desire in rapid succession because no single desire can ever be satisfied. Even when things go well there is always a nagging feeling that something is missing. A triumph is never a triumph for long. Enough is never quite enough – witness the insanity of the already super-rich doing everything they can to become even richer! Why would they do this? They do this because in the egoic world you can't be too rich or too powerful as none of those attributes, in themselves, can bring fulfillment.

But we keep trying....

The relentless treadmill of unfulfilled egoic desires has us believing that if we get that coveted job, make those extra millions, meet that perfect partner, live in that beautiful home – all will be well. Who, to one degree or another, hasn't had such expectations and then consequently experienced their emptiness and futility? Egoic life never delivers on its promise. The Buddha called this state of disillusionment 'suffering', and the objective of his 'Four Noble Truths' was to teach us how to put an end to that suffering. He recognized that there is nothing in our egoic state that can make this possible. A person may well get that job, those extra millions, that perfect partner, that fairy tale home but will STILL endure the wages of 'dukkha'. The Buddha knew this, as did Jesus Christ many years later and all the great sages since. Why then don't we give up on this mirage and ask ourselves – couldn't the opposite then be true? The answer is a resounding, YES

Dukkha evaporates and happiness increases the moment our desires and expectations decrease.

This truth is one of the cornerstones of spirituality.

And yet, in spite of the mountain of evidence that exists to support this truth, it is still our illusory egoic expectations that carry the day and continue to make the world go round. Only a gaping spiritual void can account for this striking anomaly.

Once it becomes clear that the very concept of 'winning' is an illusion, that satisfying the ego is a death trap, that we will miss the 'mark' at the end of our lives, no matter what that mark is if it depends on some form of egoic accomplishment, then that person is on the path to awareness whether he or she knows it or not. There's no need then to wade through the Bible, read the 196 'sutras' of the Buddha or spend years at the foot of a 'guru', to be at the origin of change in the world. There is certainly no harm in doing those things, but the world doesn't need enlightened beings to make a difference at this point. A little wisdom can go a long way to putting us on a sustainable path in the future and although this is not the case at present, it is feasible.

I devoted the first five chapters of this book to examining the anomalies of life in the modern world in order to highlight the factors that contribute to the paradox in the title of this book. Not a single one of those anomalies could survive even a modest emergence of wisdom in the world. For example, faced with moderation in our habits, an indifference to self-aggrandizement and a minimal sense of justice, capitalism as we know it would collapse overnight. The free-for-all of unbridled speculation we call the world of finance would cease to exist if greed was in retreat and the manic accumulation of superfluous wealth was universally spurned. The climate would change less fast and less severely if simplicity was our choice of life. The advertising industry, a toxic purveyor of harmful illusions, would be a thing of the past if the empty consumerism, vanity and insecurity on which it thrives, were to diminish. A wise person is not going to waste his or her life and that of others exchanging trivia by means of a handheld gadget they carry in their pocket. Depression, loneliness, alienation and most forms of mental illness would decrease sharply if people were to care for each other by sharing the affection, love and graciousness that all men and women possess in their spiritual essence.

The point I want to make here is that a person doesn't have to rise to the summits of spiritual development to embody qualities that would be sufficient to cause the whole edifice of 'business-as-usual' to crumble. Changes that are seemingly modest, gradual and incremental, would be far from modest in their consequences provided enough people join the movement. "You don't need to reach the end of the path to experience the benefit of walking it," as a wise soul once stated. And for this reason, it is not an entirely vain hope that change in our current trajectory is within our reach because many people have understood this. A tectonic shift in human destiny IS STILL possible. This is our only hope.

I can't terminate this book without a brief word on the enormous relevance of 'awareness' when it comes to climate change. E F Schumacher in his iconic book *Small is Beautiful* outlined the requisite qualities for a happy life and a sustainable environment. It took an economist by profession to understand that the most practical and expeditious qualities in this respect are also the most spiritual ones, hence his chapter highlighting the Buddhist economic principles of: "amazingly small means leading to extraordinarily satisfactory results." Moderation in our needs and ambitions is the cornerstone, he believed, and would have a domino effect on every other aspect of our lives.

One problem remains, however. Try as we might, we can't suddenly decide to moderate our needs and simplify our lives. It doesn't work that way, unfortunately. No amount of goodwill and right intentions will have that effect. We cannot wrest ourselves away from the attachments and illusions of the ego by an act of will alone. It requires a transformational change of heart (what the ancient Greeks called 'metanoia') for this to happen in a natural and enduring manner. There is reason to believe that this is possible. All humans possess three fundamental faculties – a heart, a soul and a conscience. When existential pressures mount, by means of these three faculties, a normally constituted person, free of serious pathologies, can attain the level of wisdom I referred to above. The more deterioration we see in the conditions of life on the planet, the more our hearts, souls and consciences will respond.

Viewed from this angle, it becomes ever clearer that our psycho/spiritual resources will be of far greater consequence in healing the wounds of the planet (and our own) than the economic and technological forces we place so much faith in. INNER growth is the only growth we will need in the years ahead.

In a message to his grandchildren, apologizing on behalf of his generation, William Ophuls wrote the following:

> So we bequeath you the monumental task of reestablishing civilization on principles that are sane, humane and ecological. And it is up to you; your elders are probably irredeemable. While we may have left you with little in the way of resources, your task is not hopeless. In the end civilization is not something material, it is spiritual. Be inspired by the beauty of the cosmos to invent a way of being devoted to feeding the soul instead of the belly. Rediscover the spiritual abundance that resides in material simplicity. Learn again that the only wealth worth having lies in the treasury of the human heart.

To which I add,

> *"New beginnings are often disguised as painful endings."* Lao Tzu

Epilogue

LETTER TO GLOBAL BRIEFING RE. THE GLOBAL PAYMENTS SUMMIT OF THE 28TH OF MAY 2023

In the GPS of the 28th of May 2023 Fareed Z. touts the formidable economic strength of the US – a leader in AI, its swift recovery from the pandemic, the worldwide dominance of its biggest banks, the hegemony of the dollar as the world's reserve currency and so on – giving the US license to play fast and loose with the debt limit. This story, however, is a yawn. The debt limit issue, although ostensibly significant, is a non-event that repeats itself with tedious regularity. After some predictable political horse trading, it is always lifted because the alternative would be unthinkable. In the meantime, the burning issue that Fareed and all serious journalists should be addressing lies elsewhere.

The existential challenge facing America is not the debt limit but the seismic disconnect between the fast-deteriorating moral and psychological health of American society and its robust economic health. Over 2000 years ago, a supremely wise individual posed the question: "What does it profit a man to gain the whole world if he loses his soul?". This question, that has not lost an ounce of its validity over time, continues to warn us of the dangers of forfeiting our souls in the quest for material gain.

Wealth bestows well-being provided it is accompanied by the human qualities we associate with having a soul. By itself, it's a well of despair. Nonetheless, this is precisely the Faustian bargain America is engaged in. Not a day goes by, as Fareed Zakaria informed us recently, without 120 people dying from gun violence in America, eleven of those being children. Mass shootings in the US are more than two a day on average prompting seven European countries to issue travel advisories. Intimately linked to this catastrophic situation we have mental health problems that are now of pandemic proportions. Loneliness and depression are experienced at one time or another by fully half the population, we are told by the surgeon-general. How much more evidence do we need that hope for America does not reside in winning the economic race with China but fighting the moral collapse that is occurring at home?

Why this situation is not being recognized as critical the way it should be is perplexing. The explanation, I believe, lies in the fact that American culture has become indistinguishable from the 24/7 propaganda machine that exists to persuade everyone in this nation that they are the fortunate beneficiaries of the most successful societal experiment in the history of the world and that the American Dream is there to prove it. Such triumphalism works well and there are many tactics involved in getting this message across. The ubiquitous use of the word 'hero' and the constant references to 'heroism' is one of them. Television advertisement is often centered around a profusion of incitements to be 'the best you can be', 'surpass your limits', 'be the hero of your own story' and so on. Hollywood also plays its part. This projection of unrealistic possibilities fuels a kind of empty optimism which is uniquely American. Nevertheless, there are limits to the efficacy of peddling such illusions. When people wake up to the fact that for the majority of them their daily struggles preclude any possibility of a 'heroic' outcome to their lives, a wave of anger and resentment ensues that carried Donald Trump (trafficking in a quite different set of lies and false hopes) all the way to the presidency in 2016. In spite of his being the most ludicrously unfit resident of the White House in American history, the possibility that he can be re-elected now looms ominously. This, too, should be a sharp reminder that something is fundamentally wrong at the core of the American experiment.

Shouldn't this corrosive situation be identified as the prime challenge of the nation, be denounced on a daily basis in the media and be the subject of continuous journalistic investigation? Shouldn't the possibility of a second round of Donald Trump's clueless despotism and the harmful effects on the fragile democracy of America be flashing a red light?

LETTER TO THE *NEW YORK TIMES* RE. DAVID BROOKS'S OPINION COLUMN OF JUNE 1ST.

On June 1st David Brooks wrote an opinion column in the *New York Times* excoriating the college admissions process as "one of the truly destructive institutions in American society." No argument with that. What surprises me is that, given the structures in place, such a seasoned journalist would expect any other outcome. In my view, he has dedicated a long and well-written article to stating the obvious.

The inequities of the CAP is just another glaring injustice among many, that derives from America being more polarized by wealth and privilege than at any time in its history. David Brooks points out that "today you don't need bloodlines stretching back to the Mayflower to have decent shot at getting into an elite school, but you do need to be born into a family with the resources to make lavish investments in your early education." Again, nothing could be less surprising. Why? "Families in the top one percent of earners were 77 times as likely to get admitted into the Ivy League as students from families making less than $30,000 a year," Brooks went on to say. As far as it goes, that says it all.

For an article like this to hold one's attention it would have to dig a little deeper into the underlying causes of this society-threatening anomaly that is not occurring in a third world country, but one of the oldest and (until recently) most respected democracies in the world. I believe the reason no established journalist wants to venture into the thickets of such a career-threatening undertaking is that it would require nothing less than the uncompromising denouncement of the culture and values of American society. That would be an act of Hara-Kiri.

The causes of these disparities are blindingly obvious, however. For everyone to have a 'fair shake' it would require the determined reduction of the extreme levels of socio-economic inequality that exist in America by significantly raising the standard of living of the bottom third of this society. This radical re-structuring requires massive tax hikes. Would this be unprecedented? The answer is, no. Postwar progressive rates of taxation in America reached a lofty 90% in the Eisenhower and Kennedy administrations. How else can you assure better schools, better housing, better healthcare, less crime and so on to those on the lowest rungs of the ladder. In the meantime, "the educated elite that doesn't know much about the rest of America," according to David Brooks, would do well to expand the horizons of their privileged education so as to better understand the travails of this underprivileged cohort of their fellow citizens.

Princeton sociologist Matthew Desmond, in his incisive, no-holds-barred book, Poverty By America gives us a grim but realistic view of what this is and it doesn't make for pretty reading. Poverty in America is the relentless interaction of intractably difficult circumstances – single parent homes, meaningless and ill-paid jobs, economic segregation, alcoholism, crime, drug abuse, inadequate healthcare etc – a doom loop from which extraction is well-nigh impossible. Furthermore, this trajectory without hope can lead to what Professors Anne Case and Angus Deaton of Princeton tragically labeled, 'Deaths of Despair'.

How can this problem be addressed? The same way it is tackled in other developed nations, by the transfer of wealth from the top, where there has never been so much (particularly in America) to the bottom, where there has never been so little for a first world nation. At the top end, the US is awash in riches. "A recent study estimates that collecting unpaid federal income taxes from the one percent – not raising their taxes just putting an end to their tax evasion – would add $175 billion to the public purse", Professor Desmond wrote in an article in the *New York Times* in March 2023. In addition, it is perfectly shameless that American billionaires pay an average of 8% tax (net of niches and loopholes) while a member of the middle-class would unavoidably pay from double to triple that rate.

Is any of this going to happen? Is fairness going to assert itself? Little to no chance, in my view. The powers that be will continue to offer up small, palliative measures, as they have always done, so as to avoid any fundamental change to the status quo. Compounding the problem is the fact that 'socialism' along European lines, the only and obvious solution, is as vehemently demonized by those who need it as those who oppose it!

In the 18th century, Benjamin Rush, one of the signers of the Declaration of Independence, predicted (with astonishing prescience) that America "would eventually fall apart in an orgy of selfishness".

That time is upon us, I fear.

Acknowledgements

I would like to express my thanks to the following authors, academics and journalists from whom I have borrowed much information and quotes in this book... Charles Hugh-Smith, Eckhart Tolle, Rupert Sheldrake, Jonah Goldberg, William Ophuls, Scott Galway, Ross Douthat, Derek Thompson, Megan Garber, Ian Bogost, Spencer Cox, Matthew Desmond, Thomas Piketty, Carol Anderson, Anne Case, Angus Deaton, Paul Krugman, Ashby Jardins, Peter Wehner, Zygmunt Bauman, Richard Sennett, Morris Berman, Jacques Barzun, David Brooks, Joel Kotkin, Egon Von Greyerz, Jacob Needleman, Sam Harris, Steve Jobs.

I am also indebted to *The New York Times*, *The Atlantic*, *Foreign Affairs* and the BBC for sources of news.

I am grateful, as always, for the help of David Greenacre in the initial editing of the book and Alan Gordon Walker, my publisher, for further editing and orchestrating its completion.

TIME IS RUNNING OUT

Reflections on the Modern World

JOHN REED

In *Time is Running Out: Reflections on the Modern World*,
John Reed presents the reader with an honest and uncompromising
appraisal of how politics, capitalism, social conditions and climate change
are interrelating so as to constitute a 'perfect storm' of challenges
that will determine the future of civilisation.

"It is not the strongest, or the most intelligent of the species
that survive. *It is the ones most adaptable to change*,"
stated Charles Darwin.

John Reed explains that 'the ones most adaptable to change' will be those
with the necessary psycho/spiritual resources. This book examines what
that means and how human consciousness must evolve to make life
sustainable in society and on the planet as a whole.

This is an important and timely polemic from the author of
Elegant Simplicity, published in 2009 and
One Mistake after Another, published in 2018.

ISBN 978 1 910074 28 2

www.umbriapress.co.uk

One Mistake after Another is the story of one baby boomer's odyssey that took him to many countries and cultures in the search for the holy grail of spiritual meaning in his life. His quest, at times, takes the form of a colourful and quixotic romp with perceptive snapshots of life in the 1960's and 1970's.

With uncompromising honesty, John Reed recounts his struggles between the 'true path' and that of personal egoism, the lure of money and 'the good life'. Many years later, the entire 'house of cards' of his material ambitions collapses around him.

Part modern-day morality play, *One Mistake after Another* is also the candid account of how the spiritual inclinations of a contemporary seeker are constantly challenged by the need to adapt to the highly secular world we live in – and, of course, his own shortcomings!

From the succession of triumphs and failures Reed describes in these pages, he emerges with a deeper understanding of his psycho/spiritual condition and the needs of the planet. Having learned from his own experience, he ends on a hopeful note. Unlike the socio-political solutions we place our faith in, only more widespread spiritual awareness, he suggests, can provide us with abiding solutions to the problems we face in the world today

ISBN 978 1 910074 18 3

www.umbriapress.co.uk

'An Indian Professor of Economics stood up at the Davos Forum some years ago and said that the emerging countries of the world should not aspire to western standards of living but that we should all learn to live in "elegant simplicity". At the time this struck me as an unusually wise statement and events since have proved it to be extremely prescient.'

In this important, challenging and timely book, John Reed makes reference to the millennial wisdom teachings of all traditions to indicate that the ego, by obscuring the need for inner change, is not only an obstacle to our survival in the future, but also to our happiness in the present. In face of the rising complexities of our modern world, the author reveals that only in inner and outer simplicity can true fulfillment be found.

By demanding less, we should be ready to give more. Instead of using nature as a dispensable commodity, we can respect our natural environment, conserve its beauty and sense our affiliation to it. By freeing ourselves from the constraints of egoism, we discover that elegant simplicity is not only a fundamental expression of our true human nature, but also a possible solution to the mounting psychological, social, economic and ecological challenges that we face in the world today.

ISBN 978 0 954127 55 8

www.umbriapress.co.uk

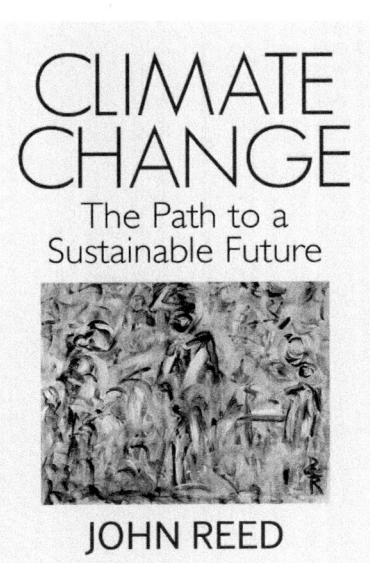

CLIMATE CHANGE
The Path to a Sustainable Future

JOHN REED

ELEGANT SIMPLICITY PART TWO

Climate change is the overriding issue of our time.
In the face of recurring climate disasters, the resistance and inertia we witness today will slowly break down. Those who have seen the writing on the wall are already choosing to change the way they live. For the young, who are mobilizing impressively, climate change is a cause of much anxiety. Sooner or later every one of us will experience the consequences of a warming planet at which time we shall all be obliged to take appropriate action. What form this will take and in what state of mind, is the real question.

The purpose of *Climate Change: The Path to a Sustainable Future* is to suggest that transitioning to an inevitable post-carbon world is not necessarily the misfortune so many fear. On the contrary, this alternative model of society offers our fragile planet, plagued by resource depletion, violence, political instability and deep socio-economic inequities a path to a new psychological, physical and morally revitalized foundation on which to build a sustainable future for mankind.

ISBN 978 1 910074 43 5

www.umbriapress.co.uk